THE POEMS OF
WILLIAM BARNES

THE POEMS OF
WILLIAM BARNES

A selection of William Barnes's Standard and Non-Standard English
poems, edited, with a critical commentary, by Valerie Shepherd.

Published by Trent Editions 1998

Trent Editions
Department of English and Media Studies
The Nottingham Trent University
Clifton Lane
Nottingham NG11 8NS

The painting on the front cover is by William Barnes and is reproduced by
permission of the Dorset County Museum.

Printed in Great Britain by Goaters, Nottingham
ISBN 0 905 48895 4

Contents

Preface and Acknowledgements

This is a thematic anthology. Its first seven sections deal in turn with the most important areas of Barnes's vision and the language of its expression. A final section then explores some intriguing resonances between Barnes and Thomas Hardy. Each section begins with a critical commentary followed by representative examples from both the Standard English and the Non-standard dialect poems (though proportionally fewer Standard poems have been included because Barnes wrote less of these and, in any case, some Standard poems are translations of an original Blackmoor version).

I am grateful to Bernard Jones for his permission to reproduce, from *The Poems of William Barnes* (Jones 1962: Carbondale, Illinois, Southern Illinois University Press), both the Standard and the Non-standard English poems included in this selection. The restoration of the grave endings (-èn), used by Barnes in his nineteenth century editions of dialect poems, has been done with Bernard Jones's encouragement. Jones's two-volume work is referenced as PWB I and PWB II in this edition.

I am also grateful to Macmillan for permission to quote the following poems from *The Complete Poems of Thomas Hardy* (Gibson 1976: London, Papermac): 'Last Signal: A Memory of William Barnes', 'The Collector Cleans his Picture', 'To a Motherless Child'.

My thanks are due to John Goodridge for his editorial support, to Elizabeth Morrish and John Goodridge for their critical advice and to Margaret Taylor for her secretarial assistance.

Bernard Jones, whose 1962 edition ensured that all of Barnes's poems were accessible and that research into his poetry could continue and develop, gave me invaluable help. His suggestions strengthened the critical commentary and in some cases saved me from error. I am immensely grateful for the benefit of his scholarship.

The front cover illustration reproduces a water colour painted by William Barnes. Its subject is the Chantry House school at Mere, which Barnes took over as a young man and which is recalled as Linden Lea in his poem 'My Orcha'd in Linden Lea'.

1. Introduction: 'A poetry of their own'

William Barnes was born in 1801 to a farming family at Bagber, near Sturminster Newton in the Dorset Vale of Blackmoor. He was a quick, intelligent pupil at the local church school and when he was about thirteen he caught the eye of a Sturminster solicitor, Mr Dashwood, and became his clerk. Later he moved to another firm of solicitors in Dorchester. Soon he would begin writing poetry, first on rather conventional subjects in the Standard English he acquired in his teens, next on rural themes, very often in the local dialect he had spoken as a child. All the time, he was reading, educating himself with the help of Dorchester Grammar School's headmaster and a local Rector. Eventually, in 1823, Barnes left Dorchester to take over a small school in Mere, Wiltshire.

He remained in Mere until 1835 when he returned to Dorchester and established another private school, for boarders and day pupils, first in Durngate Street and later at South Street. Many of his pupils would become well known and respected, like the surgeon Sir Frederick Treves, who was doctor to the Elephant Man, and the painter Joseph Clark whose work was purchased by Queen Victoria. Later, Barnes became an advocate of adult education, helping to establish the Dorchester Working Men's Mutual Improvement Society, and travelling to lecture in diverse subjects, including political and social economy, in village halls around the county. Barnes was a teacher ahead of his times for he taught by patient support, example and encouragement in an era when iron discipline and gloom tended to repress the nineteenth-century classroom. He thought that experience was as important as 'book learning' and would take his pupils out into the fields to show them plants, birds and animals. Every morning, at nine o'clock, he would demonstrate a scientific experiment, show a picture, or read a poem, and afterwards ask his class to write about what had been seen and heard. Then he would check his pupils' writing, particularly for its expression since by this time he had become an accomplished linguist.

By the end of his life Barnes not only knew more than sixty languages (writing his own diaries in Italian and German) but, as a philologist, had written many books and articles on linguistic issues including syntax, semantics and the origins of language. He had also compiled a grammar of the local

Dorset dialect whose distinctive features of lexicon and syntax he believed were particularly expressive of the local people and the labouring life that, as a professional man, he had left behind but never ceased to admire.

Yet Barnes's writing was not confined to matters of language. His wide reading made him a polymath who could write with authority on topics as diverse as maths, architecture, engineering, economics, history and folk lore. He was also a competent musician and skilled engraver. Then, in 1838, he enrolled as a part-time student of divinity — a 'ten years man' — at St John's, Cambridge, taking his BD degree in 1846. In addition, he studied for Holy Orders and was ordained as Deacon and Stipendiary Curate at Winterborne Whitcombe in 1847. For the last twenty five years of his life, after the closure of his school and until his death in 1886, Barnes was Rector of Winterborne Came, a mile or two outside Dorchester.

But, despite his busy and fulfilling professional career, and the writing of poems which were published throughout his life, his family was of the utmost importance to Barnes. When he was eighteen he saw an elegant young woman named Julia Miles stepping from a coach in the centre of Dorchester and immediately fell in love with her. Julia's father, Dorchester's Supervisor of Excise, was not impressed by this relatively poor suitor. But in 1827, after Barnes was established in the school at Mere, Mr Miles gave consent to the marriage. Barnes was devoted to Julia and their children. After his wife's death in 1852, until the end of his own life in 1886, he closed each day's entry in his diary with the Italian form of her name: 'Guilia'.

Friends, with whom he shared intellectual interests and sang and played in a chamber music group, were also of great importance to Barnes. They included Thomas Hardy, whom he first met when the younger man was working in the architect's office next door to Barnes's school in Dorchester's South Street. And then there were the remembered friends, from childhood and youth.

It is friends and family such as these, real or imagined, that are at the centre of Barnes's poetry, both the Blackmoor Vale dialect poems that he began to publish around 1834, and the Standard English poems that followed. These people and their lives form the 'good and loveworthy' (Levy 1960: 17) subjects of his work that he hoped would 'promote the innocent evening cheerfulness of the family circle on the stone floor' (Barnes 1847: 49)). He wanted, he said, to give local people 'a poetry of their own' that was 'sound, high-toned' (Barnes 1841: 510-511).

But such rural themes, as Thomas Hardy acknowledges in the introduction to his own selection from Barnes's poems (1908), were becoming anachronistic even as they were written. And Coventry Patmore argued that the poetry, even though it was conceived at a time of intense rural change and hardship, does not 'protest against anything in religion, politics, or the arrangement of society' (Patmore 1862: 155).

Andrew Motion, commenting on his own selection of Barnes's dialect poems (1994a), is more positive. He finds in the Blackmoor verse an 'urgency' of 'identification' with the concerns of local people. But, for Motion, the Standard English poems that Barnes wrote (reluctantly, after his first successes in the dialect, for he feared that readers who 'had their lots cast in town-occupations of a highly civilised community...could not sympathise with the rustic mind' (Barnes 1847: 49)) are 'pretty feeble' and 'merely sweet' (Motion 1994b: 17). However, Barnes wrote different kinds of Standard English verse. Some, written in his teens, are certainly rather mannered and conventional. A few others are translations of earlier dialect poems and these are not always successful. But most are remarkable, like the best of the Non-standard poems, for their images of vibrant colour and detail, for their subtle versification and rhythms of natural speech — and for their deep affection towards the labouring families that inhabit their landscape.

It is true that Barnes did not wish to write poetry with a 'drift' (Scott 1887: 323), by which he seems to have meant an assertive political perspective. But his prose writings, for example *Labour and Gold* (1859), deplore the impoverishment of agricultural labourers and speak out on behalf of the working class. Moreover, his poems display the kind of 'passive courage' (Hinchy 1966: 66) that Miles Barnes, William's son, recognised in his father. For, as Forsyth argues, Barnes's determined belief in the 'good and loveworthy' potential of country life may be seen not as 'a sentimental evasion of contemporary issues...[but rather as] a conscious criticism unwaveringly aimed at those very issues' (in Fletcher 1967: 138). Moreover, Barnes offered local families a sunlit landscape in poetry not as an escape from reality but, he said, as an encouragement 'to draw pure delight from the rich but frequently overlooked sources of nature within their own sphere of being' (Barnes 1847: 49).

Besides, there are also shadows on Barnes's landscape. Loss and disturbance are experienced and suffered in his poems, just as he personally suffered the loss of friends and family, the challenge of Darwinian theory to his Christian faith, the erosion of a way of life he had loved as a child, and the decline of his school after the death of his wife. But Barnes believed in fortitude and optimism, for he was certain that God's plan is good and that hardship is necessary to

...meäke us zee, if 'tis His will,
That He can bring us good vrom ill;
As after winter He do bring,
In His good time, the zunny spring,
  ('The Weather-beäten Tree'; PWB I: 152)

And so the shadows are always accepted and overcome, not only by the
people of the poems but in a sense by the poems themselves, since these
remain as a testament to a lost way of life and, in the case of the dialect
verse, as a testament to a language spoken by Barnes as a young man but
altering even as he wrote.

Yet even the dialect poems were not simply 'a poetry of their own',
a poetry for, and a memorial to the local community. They, as well as the
poems written in the Standard English that Barnes came to speak as an
adult, must also have been sustaining for Barnes himself. For he could
emulate, in the lovely images and in the careful language and structures
of his poems, the harmony and balance he found both in God's design
for the natural world and in the light and dark of human existence. And
though, at the time of his writing, Barnes was no longer a member of the
rural, labouring community, it would seem that the voice — of loving
friend, son, parent or partner in marriage — that speaks through both the
Standard and the Non-standard English poems, and revels in the memory
of past times, is his own. Hardy was surely right to observe that his friend
'often used the dramatic form of peasant speakers as a pretext for the
expression of his own mind and experience' (Hardy 1908: xi).

Yet the vision of the poems is not confined to the individual and his
local life. The love and joy it expresses in human relationships, the beauty
it reveals in the natural world, require us, as Hertz argues, to read the
poems not 'as quaint exercises in regionalism...[but as] expressions of a
universal vision' (Hertz 1985: 109-110), a vision that remains appealing
and pertinent in an age far removed from its origins in the nineteenth
century Blackmoor Vale. The sections that follow deal in turn with the
most crucial aspects of this vision and the language of its expression.

MY ORCHA'D IN LINDEN LEA

'Ithin the woodlands, flow'ry gleäded,
    By the woak tree's mossy moot,
The sheenèn grass-bleädes, timber-sheäded,
    Now do quiver under voot;
An' birds do whissle over head,
An' water's bubblèn in its bed,
An' there vor me the apple tree
Do leän down low in Linden Lea.

When leaves that leätely wer a-springèn
    Now do feäde 'ithin the copse,
An' païnted birds do hush their zingèn
    Up upon the timber's tops;
An' brown-leav'd fruit's a-turnèn red,
In cloudless zunsheen, over head,
Wi' fruit vor me, the apple tree
  Do leän down low in Linden Lea.

Let other vo'k meäke money vaster
    In the aïr o' dark-room'd towns,
I don't dread a peevish meäster;
    Though noo man do heed my frowns,
I be free to goo abrode,
Or teäke ageän my hwomeward road
To where, vor me, the apple tree
Do leän down low in Linden Lea.

WOODLEY

Sweet Woodley! oh! how fresh an' gaÿ
Thy leänes an' vields be now in Maÿ,
The while the broad-leav'd clotes do zwim
In brooks wi' gil'cups at the brim;
An' yollow cowslip-beds do grow
By thorns in blooth so white as snow;
An' win' do come vrom copse wi' smells
O' grægles wi' their hangèn bells!

Though time do dreve me on, my mind
Do turn in love to thee behind,
The seäme's a bulrush that's a-shook
By wind a-blowèn up the brook:
The curlèn stream would dreve en down,
But plaÿsome aïr do turn en roun',
An' meäke en seem to bend wi' love
To zunny hollows up above.

Thy tower still do overlook
The woody knaps an' windèn brook,
An' leäne's wi' here an' there a hatch,
An' house wi' elem-sheäded thatch,
An' vields where chaps do vur outdo
The Zunday sky, wi' cwoats o' blue;
An' maïdens' frocks do vur surpass
The whitest deäsies in the grass.

What peals to-day from thy wold tow'r
Do strike upon the zummer flow'r,
As all the club, wi' dousty lags,
Do walk wi' poles an' flappèn flags,
An' wind, to music, roun' between
A zwarm o' vo'k upon the green!
Though time do dreve me on, my mind
Do turn wi' love to thee behind.

VOK A-COMÈN INTO CHURCH

The church do zeem a touchèn zight,
    When vo'k, a-comèn in at door,
    Do softly tread the long-aïl'd vloor
Below the pillar'd arches' height,
    Wi' bells a-pealèn,
    Vo'k a-kneelèn,
Hearts a-healèn, wi' the love
An' peace a-zent em vrom above.

An' there, wi' mild an' thoughtvul feäce,
　　Wi' downcast eyes, an' vaïces dum',
　　The wold an' young do slowly come,
An' teäke in stillness each his pleäce,
　　　A-zinkèn slowly,
　　　Kneelèn lowly,
Seekèn holy thoughts alwone,
In praÿ'r avore their Meäker's throne.

An' there be sons in youthvul pride,
　　An' fathers weak wi' years an' païn,
　　An' daughters in their mother's traïn,
The tall wi' smaller at their zide;
　　　Heads in murnèn
　　　Never turnèn,
Cheäks a-burnèn, wi' the het
O' youth, an' eyes noo tears do wet.

There friends do settle, zide by zide,
　　The knower speechless to the known;
　　Their vaïce is there vor God alwone;
To flesh an' blood their tongues be tied.
　　　Grief a-wringèn,
　　　Jaÿ a-zingèn,
Praÿr a-bringèn welcome rest
So softly to the troubled breast.

THE RWOSE IN THE DARK

In zummer, leäte at evenèn tide,
　　I zot to spend a moonless hour
'Ithin the window, wi' the zide
　　A-bound wi' rwoses out in flow'r,
Bezide the bow'r, vorsook o' birds,
An' listen'd to my true-love's words.

A-risèn to her comely height,
　　She push'd the swingèn ceäsement round;
And I could hear, beyond my zight,
　　The win'-blow'd beech-tree softly sound,

On higher ground, a-swaÿen slow,
On drough my happy hour below.

An' tho' the darkness then did hide
    The dewy rwose's blushèn bloom,
He still did cast sweet aïr inside
    To Jeäne, a-chattèn in the room;
An' though the gloom did hide her feäce,
Her words did bind me to the pleäce.

An' there, while she, wi' runnèn tongue,
    Did talk unzeen 'ithin the hall,
I thought her like the rwose that flung
    His sweetness vrom his darken'd ball,
'Ithout the wall, an' sweet's the zight
Ov her bright feäce by mornèn light.

A WIFE A-PRAÏS'D

'Twer Maÿ, but ev'ry leaf wer dry
All day below a sheenèn sky;
    The zun did glow wi' yollow gleäre,
    An' cowslips blow wi' yollow gleäre,
Wi' graegles' bells a-droopèn low,
An' bremble boughs a-stoopèn low;
    While culvers in the trees did coo
        Above the vallèn dew.

An' there, wi' heäir o' glossy black,
Bezide your neck an' down your back,
    You rambled gaÿ a-bloomèn feäir;
    By boughs o' maÿ a-bloomèn feäir;
An' while the birds did twitter nigh,
An' water weäves did glitter nigh,
    You gather'd cowslips in the lew,
        Below the vallèn dew.

An' now, while you've a-been my bride
As years o' flow'rs ha' bloom'd an' died,

Your smilèn feäce ha' been my jaÿ;
Your soul o' greäce ha' been my jaÿ;
An' wi' my evenèn rest a-come,
An' zunsheen to the west a-come,
I'm glad to teäke my road to you
    Vrom vields o' vallèn dew.

An' when the raïn do wet the maÿ,
A-bloomèn where we woonce did straÿ,
An' win' do blow along so vast,
An' streams do flow along so vast;
Ageän the storms so rough abroad,
An' angry tongues so gruff abroad,
The love that I do meet vrom you
    Is lik' the vallèn dew.

An' you be sprack's a bee on wing,
In search ov honey in the Spring:
The dawn-red sky do meet ye up;
The birds vu'st cry do meet ye up;
An' wi' your feäce a-smilèn on,
An' busy hands a-tweilèn on,
You'll vind zome usevul work to do
    Until the vallèn dew.

THE COMMON A-TOOK IN

Oh! no, Poll, no! Since they've a-took
The common in, our lew wold nook
Don't seem a bit as used to look
    When we had runnèn room;
Girt banks do shut up ev'ry drong,
An' stratch wi' thorny backs along
Where we did use to run among
    The vuzzen an' the broom.

Ees; while the ragged colts did crop
The nibbled grass, I used to hop
The emmet-buts, vrom top to top,
    So proud o' my spry jumps:

Wi' thee behind or at my zide,
A-skippèn on so light an' wide
'S thy little frock would let thee stride,
    Among the vuzzy humps.

Ah while the lark up over head
Did twitter, I did search the red
Thick bunch o' broom, or yollow bed
    O' vuzzen vor a nest;
An' thou di'st hunt about, to meet
Wi' strawberries so red an' sweet,
Or clogs or shoes off hosses veet,
    Or wild thyme vor thy breast;

Or when the cows did run about
A-stung, in zummer, by the stout,
Or when they plaÿ'd, or when they foüght,
    Di'st stand a-lookèn on:
An' where white geese, wi' long red bills,
Did veed among the emmet-hills,
There we did goo to vind their quills
    Alongzide o' the pon'.

What fun there wer among us, when
The haÿward come, wi' all his men,
To drève the common, an' to pen
    Strange cattle in the pound;
The cows did bleäre, the men did shout
An' toss their eärms an' sticks about,
An' vo'ks, to own their stock, come out
    Vrom all the housen round.

HAÿ-MEÄKEN

'Tis merry ov a zummer's day,
Where vo'k be out a-meäkèn haÿ;
Where men an' women, in a string,
Do ted or turn the grass, an' zing,

Wi' cheemèn vaïces, merry zongs,
A-tossèn o' their sheenèn prongs
Wi' eärms a-zwangèn left an' right,
In colour'd gowns an' shirtsleeves white;
Or, wider spread, a-reäkèn round
The rwosy hedges o' the ground,
Where Sam do zee the speckled sneäke,
An' try to kill en wi' his reäke;
An' Poll do jump about an' squall,
To zee the twistèn slooworm crawl.

'Tis merry where a gaÿ-tongued lot
Ov haÿ-meäkers be all a-squot,
On lightly-russlèn haÿ, a-spread
Below an elem's lofty head,
To rest their weary limbs an' munch
Their bit o' dinner, or their nunch;
Where teethy reäkes do lie all round
By picks a-stuck up into ground.
An' wi' their vittles in their laps,
An' in their hornen cups their draps
O' cider sweet, or frothy eäle,
Their tongues do run wi' joke an' teäle.

An' when the zun, so low an' red,
Do sheen above the leafy head
O' zome broad tree, a-rizèn high
'Avore the vi'ry western sky,
'Tis merry where all han's do goo
Athirt the groun', by two an' two,
A-reäkèn, over humps an' hollors,
The russlèn grass up into rollers.
An' woone do row it into line,
An' woone do clwose it up behine;
An' after them the little bwoys
Do stride an' fling their eärms all woys,
Wi' busy picks, an' proud young looks
A-meäkèn up their tiny pooks.
An' zoo 'tis merry out among
The vo'k in haÿ-vield all day long.

SCHOOL FEAST

ELDERS

We thank Thee Lord this happy day
For this Thy children's food and play.
We give Thee thanks for all the names
Now gather'd here in childhood's games.

GIRLS

We girls give thanks for all our joy.

BOYS

And we are thankful, every boy.

ELDERS

We thank all those who kindly stored
With these good things the children's board.
We thank the friends who give us here
Unstinted gifts of goodly cheer.

GIRLS

We girls give thanks for drink and meat.

BOYS

We boys give thanks for this good treat.

ELDERS

We thank the friends whose hands outbear
To ev'ry child his goodly share,
All those whose feet here step or stand
With drink and meat for every hand.

GIRLS

We girls give thanks, both tall and small.

BOYS

We boys bethank them, one and all.

ELDERS

We thank Thee, Lord, for Thy good word.
For Thy good schools we thank Thee Lord.
We thank Thee for Thy light and truth
Thus given us in early youth.

GIRLS
O keep us Lord from ev'ry ill.

BOYS
O keep us as Thy children still.

SHELTER

Not joyless is wind, raving high
    Above many-wav'd streams by the hill;
While the clouds swiftly rush o'er the sky
    Behind trees with no limb that is still,
If we only can stand, and withstand
The wild storm as it sweeps o'er the land.

Not joyless where rain, on the blast
    Of highwind, rushes on like a smoke;
And the raindrops, like gunshots, are cast
    On the pond out below the bare oak,
If we walk not in clothing too thin
To keep warm from the rain the white skin.

Yet good to a shelter to flee;
    To a nook in a hollow-cut rick;
Or the cove of an old hollow tree,
    Or the wall-hooding ivy, wall-thick,
Or the bird boy's turf hut, weather proof
To the wind, and the rain, wall and roof.

HOME

With the sun glowing warm at its height,
And the people at work in white sleeves,
And the gold-banded bee in its flight,
With the quick-flitting birds among leaves:
There my two little children would run,
And would reach and would roll in their fun,
And would clasp in their hands,

Stick or stone for their play, —
In their hands, that but little had grown;
For their play, with a stick or a stone.

As the sun from his high summer bow
Had begun o'er the orchard to fall,
There he left the brown beehives, in row,
In the shade of the houses grey wall;
And the flowers, outshining in bloom,
Some in light, and some others in gloom,
To the cool of the air,
    And the damp of the dew,—
The air, from the apple-tree shades,
And the dew, on the grasses' green blades.

And there was my orchard well-tined
With a hedge and a steep-sided bank,
Where ivy had twin'd on the rind
Of the wood-stems, and trees in high rank,
To keep out the wide lipped cow,
And the stiff-snouted swine, that would plough
Up the soft-bladed grass,
    By the young apple-trees,—
The grass, that had grown a good height,
And the trees, that in blossom were white.

O when is a father's good time,
That will yield to his toil the best joy?
Is it when he is spending his prime
For his children, the girl and the boy?
Or when they have grown to their height,
And are gone from his hearing and sight,
And their mother's one voice
    Is left home at the door,—
A voice, that no longer may sing,
At the door, that more seldom may swing?

2. 'The good and the loveworthy'

Barnes believed that his poems had a didactic purpose. Amongst his papers, now kept in the Dorchester County Museum, is a note defining the purpose of 'Poetry' and sub-titled 'Teaching'. It reads:

> Steering and guiding the soul to setting forth the good and loveworthy that men's minds would more readily take and hold it.
> (Levy 1960: 17)

Given their educational objective, Barnes intended that his poetic images and their presentation should be 'high toned'. They should 'light up [the countryside's] more lovely features, foster its better feelings and tastes and touch its soul with the sweet pastoral spirit' (Barnes 1841: 510-511). Consequently his poems shine with the light of the sun as it warms yellow fields, clear blue streams, and butterflies resting in the sweet smelling gardens in which workers rest at the end of the day.

Massingham was therefore right to observe that 'all the graciousness and greenness and floweriness of the Dorset pastures is in Barnes'. But he was incorrect to claim that 'all that lives upon them' is also there (Massingham 1942: 408). Barnes himself acknowledged that the people in his poems represented those 'somewhat above the average' in his community (Dugdale: 227). And, unlike his near contemporary, John Clare, he did not write of the countryside's untamed animals like the badger, the vixen, the mole, the hedgehog. Snakes do appear in Barnes's work but only as harmless players in the country scene ('Haÿ-Meäken'; PWB I: 114; 'The Common a-took in'; PWB I: 158). Nor does Barnes describe labouring on the land in precise or rugged detail, unlike Bloomfield, whose work, published earlier in the century, aimed to be 'experimentally true' (Unwin 1954: 93). But then, the adult Barnes, as schoolmaster and parson, was an observer rather than a participant in landwork. Bloomfield's description of butter making is exact, technical and without sentiment:

> Slow rolls the churn, its load of clogging cream
> At once forgoes its quality and name;
> From knotty particles first floating wide
> Congealing butter's dash'd from side to side;
> (Lawson 1971:15)

Barnes's vision of the dairy, however, focuses on the moral excellence of the milkmaid's industry, merely sketching in the detail of her labours, concentrating these on the attractive colour of the scene as it is appreciated by an onlooker.

> An' Poll don't zit up half the night,
>   Nor lie vor half the day a-bed;
> An' zoo her eyes be sparklèn bright,
>   An' zoo her cheäks be bloomèn red.

> An' she, at mornèn an' at night,
>   Do skim the yollow cream, an' mwold
> An' wring her cheeses red an' white,
>   An' zee the butter vetch'd an' roll'd.
>   ('The Milk-Maïd o' the Farm', verses 2, 7; PWB I: 180)

Even those poems which acknowledge the changes of an industrial century are firmly linked to Barnes's concept of a 'loveworthy' rural life. There are, for example, two poems called 'The Raïlroad' (PWB I: 309, 309), but though both of these begin with the speed and noise and steam of the train, they end by focusing on God's consistent love or the rewards of goodness.

Another train takes the local miller, John Bloom, to London to see the Crystal Palace Exhibition ('John Bloom in Lon'on', PWB I: 473). Bloom is a 'worthy' man — 'Noo stings o' conscience ever broke / His rest' — and very large: 'Athirt the chest he wer so wide / As two or dree ov me or you'. In fact, he is so big that he cannot fit into a cab when he arrives in the city. '"Girt lump"', the cab driver cries. '"Who is the man?"' onlookers shout. Unembarrassed, Bloom calls back, '"A halfstarv'd Do'set man"', evidently ridiculing with sarcasm a city view of impoverished and sickly country existence.

Images such as these may strike the modern reader as a patronising falsification of harsh nineteenth century rural conditions. Certainly Robert Young's roughly contemporaneous poetry (1868) laments Dorset rural trials and escape from them through drink. But this is not the vision of Barnes's poems. And the well being of his rural personae, like Bloom, has a basis in fact, for Bernard Jones has pointed out that industrial town doctors of the 1830s and 40s described the health of manual workers in heavy industry as inferior to that of farm workers. It is true, however, that the community represented in Barnes's work seems historically to belong to the days of his own boyhood and many of its activities seem to be a revitalisation of his own carefree experiences before the century's changes disrupted the community. Consequently, Barrell and Bull have argued that Barnes's vision is 'too nostalgic to be at all serviceable' (1982: 431). But serviceable in what way and to whom? Barnes's poems did not by any means alienate contemporary local audiences. His daughter, Lucy Baxter, witnessed one of his poetry readings at the Dorchester Town Hall and wrote (under the pseudonym, Scott):

> It seemed...that the crowd of human beings was a magic harp on which [he] played, bringing forth at his will the emotions he chose. If this seems exaggerated, let it be remembered that it was the first time a Dorset audience had heard its feeling, language, and daily life portrayed in its own common speech, and the effect was all the greater from the newness of the emotion. (Scott 1887: 167)

This enthusiasm is confirmed by readers themselves. In 1869 Barnes received a letter from an old domestic servant, brought up in Dorset but now working in London. She wrote that, whilst dusting books from a sale, she had discovered a volume of his poems.

> Sir, I shook hands with you in my heart, and I laughed and cried by turns. The old home of my youth and all my dear ones now mouldering in the earth came back to mind. (Barnes's papers in Dorset County Museum: Vol 4, 42)

Barnes would have been gratified that he had succeeded in his intention to encourage readers 'to contemplate the charms of rural nature' (Barnes 1841: 510-511). At the same time, his prose writings — including articles in the Poole Herald during 1848, called 'Humilis Domus: Some Thoughts on the Abodes, Live and Social Conditions of the Poor, especially in Dorsetshire', in which he called for a lessening of the labourer's 'excessive daily toil' — show that he recognised and was distressed by agrarian poverty. 'There is a social disease among us and who would not wish to find its origin', he wrote (Barnes 1849: 54). But Barnes's own peaceful and conservative personality would not incite readers of his poems to try to change the structures of their often hard lives. He could do nothing but try for its amelioration through fostering the psychology not of outward challenge and conflict but of patient acceptance and the preservation of an inner self-respect. Max Keith Sutton sees Barnes's pastoral as 'a way of dealing with reality, not of avoiding it' (Hardin 1979: 34). Indeed, Sutton is critical of Raymond Williams's slighting of evidence that rural people could have been contented. He cites Williams's selection of harsh details from an autobiography whilst ignoring the writer's assertion that he was 'perfectly happy' and he suggests that 'with all its hardships, rural life has afforded surprising possibilities of happiness, and pastoral writing may be truthful in representing good times as well as bad' (Hardin 1979: 39-40).

Barnes's poems certainly represent the good times, although, as will be explained, his landscape is not entirely without shadow. This landscape is full of people. Though his poems describe the land as it changes through the seasons, almost all, after his very early Standard English verses, are spoken by a local persona or refer to local personalities whose living is closely connected with the land.

These individuals are seen as members of groups. They belong to a family, as husband, wife or child. And they are part of the wider village community as squire, worker or friend. The keynote of behaviour within and between these groups is support and co-operation. At Christmas and other times of celebration, the Squire provides hospitality for the community.

> Zoo then the leädy an' the squier,
>   At Chris'mas, gather'd girt an' small,
> Vor me'th, avore their roarèn vier,
>   An' roun' their bwoard, 'ithin the hall;
> An' there, in glitt'rèn rows, between
> The roun'-rimm'd pleätes, our knives did sheen,
>   Wi' frothy eäle, an' cup an' can,
>   Vor maïd an' man, at Herrenston.
> ('Herrènston'; PWB I: 340)

There is also, amongst the labouring families, supportive interaction of the kind described in 'See-Saw'. The poem begins from the simple action of borrowing and lending tea. But it extends to a consideration of mutual help, based on childhood games of see-saw.

> At see-saw, see-saw, I and you
> Would always make the fellow two.

Each helped the other to tip the balance, but it was a pragmatic assistance, because

> Some evil day, if I let you
> Fall down, why, I may tumble too.
>   ('See-saw: A housewife to a neighbour'; PWB II: 836)

The see-saw metaphor is no doubt based on games remembered from Barnes's childhood, and children themselves are frequently the subject of a poem. Mostly these children are playing, unfettered by 'city primness' and enjoying the freedom that 'let them loose to tread / The yellow cowslip's downcast head' ('Rustic Childhood'; PWB II: 643). However, even as they play, they are learning the adult role of industrious worker that Barnes regarded as not merely economically but, most importantly, as physically, morally and emotionally rewarding. In the fields of his poems

...the little bwoys
Do stride an' fling their eärms all woys,
Wi' busy picks, an' proud young looks
A-meäkèn up their tiny pooks.
('Haÿ-Meäken'; PWB I: 114)

Whenever possible the play turns into a real contribution to the family's labouring life. Father may bid his children to

...heal young beäns or peas in line,
Or tie em up wi' rods an' twine,
Or peel a kindly withy white
To hold a droopèn flow'r upright.
('Eclogue: The Bit o' Ground at Hwome'; PWB I: 345)

Little disturbs these children's days, except perhaps a mild argument with another child, as in 'False Friends-like' (PWB I: 329) when a boy tips a younger child from his wheelbarrow into a puddle.

As they grow older, Barnes's young men and women remain energetic and retain the playful, innocent air of their childhoods. They do not, unlike his friend Thomas Hardy's fictional Jude, strain for a life beyond their village. They are boisterous in 'Out A-Nuttèn' (PWB I: 148) or 'Teäkèn in Apples' (PWB I: 150). They flirt in 'Bit O' Sly Coortèn' (PWB I: 95), enjoying a 'love that burn'd but thought noo harm' ('The Girt Woak Tree that's in the Dell'; PWB I: 81). But though there is an occasional reference to an illegitimate child and a girl ruined by her lover's desertion and family's rejection (as in 'The Weepèn Leädy'; PWB I: 170), the history and the consequences of these traumas are barely sketched. Instead, the family lives of these young people, when they are grown up and fulfilled as husbands, wives and parents, is a central theme of the poems.

For Barnes, man and woman contributed in different but equal measure to marriage.

Do not begin with the thought that the minds of man and woman are of the same cast, or that one is higher than the other; neither is the higher, but they differ that each may be the best for its mission, and each has that which the other lacks, and both make together the one full mind of mankind. (Dugdale 1953: 145)

The mission of these men and women is essentially to live the working life they have watched and emulated in play since childhood. Keeping an eye on his children nearby, a father works in the fields, repairs his home and tends his garden. The mother works on the land too, mowing, haymaking, milking, but at the same time she teaches her child — like the 'Mother o' Mothers' who passed on traditional values as she told 'teäles o' vorgotten wold vo'k' and, encouraging language, 'worded [his] own little tongue' (PWB I: 510).

Yet, though mother and father are both individuals, defined by a number of experiences including their separate work and their separate parenthood, it is their roles in combination that Barnes emphasises most in his poetry of a co-operative community. For the family together is his epitome of the good and the loveworthy. Though it is one husband's 'set time vor to goo / To the grist-mill out at Sherbrook under Bere', he is equally concerned to arrange that his wife and children should be able to meet him on the way home.

> At the time, then, I've a -twold ye, you mid hear
> My two wheel rims come a-spinnen on the road,
> An' the spring cart wi' the seat up shall be leer
> To teäke you, Jeäne, an' the childern vor his lwoad.
> Zoo come out, then, to the zun
> Wi the youngsters vor a run,
> Come an' meet me, wi' the childern, on the road.
> ('Come an' Meet me wi' the Childern on the Road'; PWB I: 532)

When these children grow up and marry in their turn, father and mother can 'teäke a sweetheart's walk woonce mwore'. Barnes acknowledges that their family life has had its share of 'ceäres' that 'meäde our life so black'. Yet these are

> ...now a-lost behind our back.
> Zoo never mwope, in midst of hope,
> To slight our blessèns would be sin.
> ('Married Peäir's Love Walk'; PWB I: 331)

Indeed, Barnes's poems insist that, because 'God's love is steadvast', 'He'll gi'e us mwore than he do teäke' ('Rivers Don't Gi'e Out'; PWB I: 112). Families are united by their belief in God, the Church and its tradition. The church building and its services are both a 'meäns o' grace' and the firm centre of village life, offering relief from the week's 'ceare an' tweil' and providing the focal point for local society that 'The Church an' Happy Zunday' demonstrates.

> 'Tis good to zee woone's naïghbours come
> Out drough the churchyard, vlockèn hwome,
> (PWB I: 193)

This focal point connects the family generations, as 'Lydlinch Bells' proclaims.

> There sons did pull the bells that rung
> Their mothers' weddèn peals avore,
> The while their fathers led em young
> An' blushèn vrom the churches door
> (PWB I: 302)

In fact, continuity in a cultivated and controlled environment is at the heart of Barnes's 'good and loveworthy' vision. There is a contrast here between Barnes and his near-contemporary, John Clare. As Massingham points out, Clare 'spoke for the country that had made the husbandman' whereas Barnes wrote of 'the countryman who has remade nature' (Massingham 1942: 408). For Barnes, people create the landscape and its atmosphere. 'Our Fathers' Works' (PWB I: 270) praises the roads, churches, mills and landworks that previous generations have built, shaping the environment and, thereby, the families that live and labour within it. The buildings, rising and blending with the land, are made not only by human hands but also by human relationships, for a new house is lacking unless

> ...friends, when you do roam,
> Come to zee us, come at whiles,
> Wi' your looks, an' words, an' smiles,
> We shall veel the mwore at hwome.
> ('The New House'; PWB I:497)

For Barnes, this remaking of the landscape and the life upon it is not a difficult job. Nature, for him, is tractable. There is a God-given 'fitness' in all things. There is 'fitness of water to irrigate growth, and to run for all lips to the sea, fitness of land to take and send onward the stream' (Barnes 1861: 133). Trees are always 'good company' ('Trees be Company'; PWB I: 312), the cow is patient with the milkmaid — she would 'never overzet her païl; / Nor try to kick her nimble hand' ('The Milk-Maïd o' the Farm'; PWB I: 80). Very occasionally the weather challenges humanity. The wind is 'wild-reäven', rocking the elms and driving the waves in 'Jenny Out Vrom Hwome' (PWB I: 145) — but it is significant that Jenny *is* away from the calm and contented landscape that is her home in Barnes's poetry.

However, 'The Zilver-Weed' acknowledges a poignant balance in the relationship with nature that the people of Barnes's vision set out to control and cultivate (PWB I: 434). The zilver-weed could not grow whilst a father's children played and trampled it with their 'litty steps'; but at the same time his older girls made sure the family's roses were 'all a-trimm'd an' traïn'd'. Now that the children have grown and moved away, however, the zilver-weed can thrive — but the rose trees, no longer cared for, 'woone by woone...do die, / An' vew of all the row do stand'.

The shadow that darkens this poem is replicated in much of Barnes's work. Change and loss, of friends, family, tradition and of self-sufficient wellbeing, are never far from his sunlit vision. After all, he had known personal loss. His mother died whilst he was very young, he was separated from Julia for some time during their courtship, and one of their sons died as a small boy. Besides, he witnessed everyday disruption and tragedy all around him. There is the wrench of parting in a daughter marrying and leaving home, as 'Jeäne's Weddèn Day in Mornèn' describes (PWB I: 111), and there is the much greater pain, told in 'The Dree Woaks', of a daughter dying (PWB I: 214). The loss of a partner is the subject of 'The Rwose that Deck'd her Breast' (PWB I: 198). Barnes was also well aware of the destructive effects of nineteenth century economic changes, for his own father and uncle had lost land. His writing recognises the consequences of these developments to tradition and family life, particularly through a number of eclogues: 'Two Farms in Woone' (PWB I: 160) describes the effects of engrossing, 'The Common a-took In' (PWB I: 158) deals with enclosure, 'Rusticus Emigrans' (PWB I: 482) is about emigration. And whilst the labouring family is hit by these alterations to a way of life, the farmer of the new economy ploughs up every available bit of land. 'What's zwold an' bought / Is all that is worthy o' thought' ('The Leäne'; PWB I: 306).

But always the people of Barnes's poems accept and cope with whatever troubles they face. 'The Common a-took In' (PWB I: 158) regrets enclosure, yet it dwells not on a sense of exclusion but upon the remembered joy of the once open fields, upon children jumping and skipping, searching for bird's nests and strawberries. In 'The Rwose that Deck'd her Breast' (PWB I: 198) Jenny has lost her husband after two years of marriage, but she has comfort and pleasure in his baby. In 'The Wife a-lost' (PWB I: 333) a widower carries on with life, not evading his sorrow but mitigating his pain by avoiding places in which he has been happy with his wife. Besides, he looks forward to being reunited with her, 'Where you be gone avore, / An' be a-waïtèn vor me now, / To come vor evermwore'. Barnes's confidence in God's goodness and support resonates throughout his poems, accepting His plan and relying on His care. Jeännet's death in 'The Dree Woaks' (PWB I: 111) is accepted as God's will. Richard, in 'Rusticus Emigrans', (PWB I: 482) fears separation from the land on which he has worked and raised his family, but the poem ends in reliance upon God: 'If we do do our best he woon't forsiake us'.

The Standard English poems, written after Barnes's first successful poems in the local dialect, share the 'good and loveworthy' landscape of the Non-standards, including its shadows. But, in addition, they occasionally display signs of Barnes the scholar, dealing as in 'Learning' (PWB II: 692) and 'Architecture' (PWB II: 696) with themes from his professional life. Moreover, 'Architecture' is a sonnet and there are no sonnets at all in Barnes's Blackmoor dialect poems. Yet this omission need not imply that he thought the genre, with its potential for controlled, intellectual argument, less appropriate for Non-standard than Standard English, for nor are there any sonnets in the Standard poems published after 1846. Moreover, all the sonnets that Barnes did write resist the potential for debate that lies in their characteristic thesis and antithesis: both the Standard and the Non-standard poems, whatever their form, are uncomplicated in their thought.

They all, however, resonate with a profound affection for their subjects. Barnes believed that 'there can be no art without love' (Barnes 1861:126) and love, he claimed, inspired his work: 'my heart did kindle wi' the fleäme o't, / Whenever I did zee a touchen zight' ('The Young Rhymer Snubbed'; PWB I: 493). That love is expressed in the approval Barnes bestows on the labouring families of his landscape, in the delight manifested in their description, in the gentle light that reveals the clear, vibrant colour of his images. There was not, he said, 'a line which was not inspired by love for and kindly sympathy with the things and people described' (Kilvert 1944: 242-243).

THE ZUMMER HEDGE

As light do gleäre in ev'ry ground,
Wi' boughy hedges out a-round
A-climmèn up the slopèn brows
O' hills, in rows o' sheädy boughs:
The while the hawthorn buds do blow
As thick as stars, an' white as snow;
Or cream-white blossoms be a-spread
About the guelder-rwoses' head;
How cool's the sheäde, or warm's the lewth,
Bezide a zummer hedge in blooth.

When we've a-work'd drough longsome hours,
Till dew's a-dried vrom dazzlèn flow'rs,
The while the climmèn zun ha' glow'd
Drough mwore than half his daily road:
Then where the sheädes do slily pass
Athirt our veet upon the grass,
As we do rest by lofty ranks
Ov elems on the flow'ry banks;
How cool's the sheäde, or warm's the lewth,
Bezide a zummer hedge in blooth.

But oh! below woone hedge's zide
Our jaÿ do come a'most to pride;
Out where the high-stemm'd trees do stand,
In row bezide our own free land,
An' where the wide-leav'd clote mid zwim
'Ithin our water's rushy rim:
An' raïn do vall, an' zuns do burn,
An' each in season, and in turn,
To cool the sheäde or warm the lewth
Ov our own zummer hedge in blooth.

How soft do sheäke the zummer hedge—
How soft do swaÿ the zummer zedge—
How bright be zummer skies an' zun—
How bright the zummer brook do run;
An' feäir the flow'rs do bloom, to feäde

Behind the swaÿen mower's bleäde;
An' sweet be merry looks o' jaÿ,
By weäles an' pooks o' June's new haÿ,
Wi' smilèn age, an laughèn youth,
Bezide the zummer hedge in blooth.

THE RAÏLROAD I

I took a flight, awhile agoo,
Along the raïls, a stage or two,
An' while the heavy wheels did spin
An' rottle, wi a deafnèn din,
In clouds o' steam, the zweepèn traïn
Did shoot along the hill bound plaïn,
As sheädes o' birds in flight, do pass
Below em on the zunny grass.
An' as I zot, an' look'd abrode
On leänen land an' windèn road,
The ground a-spread along our flight
Did vlee behind us out o' zight;
The while the zun, our heav'nly guide,
Did ride on wi' us, zide by zide.
An' zoo, while time, vrom stage to stage,
Do car us on vrom youth to age,
The e'thly pleasures we do vind
Be soon a-met, an' left behind;
But God, beholdèn vrom above
Our lowly road, wi' yearnèn love,
Do keep bezide us, stage by stage,
Vrom be'th to youth, vrom youth to age.

JOHN BLOOM IN LON'ON

(All true)

John Bloom he wer a jolly soul,
    A grinder o' the best o' meal,
Bezide a river that did roll,
    Vrom week to week, to push his wheel.

His flour wer all a-meäde o' wheat;
An' fit for bread that vo'k mid eat;
Vor he would starve avore he'd cheat.
"'Tis pure," woone woman cried;
"Aye, sure," woone mwore replied;
"You'll vind it nice. Buy woonce, buy twice,"
Cried worthy Bloom the miller.

Athirt the chest he wer so wide
 As two or dree ov me or you.
An' wider still vrom zide to zide,
 An' I do think still thicker drough.
Vall down, he coulden, he did lie
When he wer up on zide so high
As up on end or perty nigh.
"Meäke room," woone naïghbour cried;
"'Tis Bloom," woone mwore replied;
"Good morn t'ye all, bwoth girt an' small,"
Cried worthy Bloom the miller.

Noo stings o' conscience ever broke
 His rest, a-twitèn o'n wi' wrong,
Zoo he did sleep till mornèn broke,
 An' birds did call en wi' their zong.
But he did love a harmless joke,
An' love his evenèn whiff o' smoke,
A-zittèn in his cheäir o' woak.
"Your cup," his daughter cried;
"Vill'd up," his wife replied;
"Aye, aye; a drap avore my nap,"
Cried worthy Bloom the miller.

When Lon'on vok did meäke a show
 O' their girt glassen house woone year,
An' people went, bwoth high an' low,
 To zee the zight, vrom vur an' near,
"O well," cried Bloom, "why I've a right
So well's the rest to zee the zight;
I'll goo, an' teäke the raïl outright."

"Your feäre," the booker cried;
"There, there," good Bloom replied;
"Why this June het do meäke woone zweat,"
Cried worthy Bloom the miller,

Then up the guard did whissle sh'ill,
      An' then the engine pank'd a-blast,
An' rottled on so loud's a mill,
      Avore the traïn, vrom slow to vast.
An' oh! at last how they did spank
By cuttèn deep, an' high-cast bank
The while their iron ho'se did pank.
"Do whizzy", woone o'm cried;
"I'm dizzy," woone replied;
"Aye, here's the road to hawl a lwoad,"
Cried worthy Bloom the miller.

In Lon'on John zent out to call
      A tidy trap, that he mid ride
To zee the glassen house, an' all
      The lot o' things a-stow'd inside.
"Here, Boots, come here," cried he, "I'll dab
A sixpence in your han' to nab
Down street a tidy little cab."
"A feäre," the boots then cried;
"I'm there," the man replied.
"The glassen pleäce, your quickest peäce,"
Cried worthy Bloom the miller.

The steps went down wi' rottlèn slap,
      The zwingèn door went open wide:
Wide? no; vor when the worthy chap
      Stepp'd up to teäke his pleäce inside,
Breast-foremost, he wer twice too wide
Vor thik there door. An' then he tried
To edge in woone an' tother zide.
"'Twont do," the drever cried;
"Can't goo," good Bloom replied;
"That you should bring theäse vooty thing!"
Cried worthy Bloom the miller.

"Come," cried the drever. "Pay your feäre;
    You'll teäke up all my time, good man."
"Well," answer'd Bloom, "to meäke that square,
    You teäke up me, then, if you can."
"I come at call," the man did nod.
"What then?" cried Bloom, "I han't a-rod,
An' can't in thik there hodmadod."
"Girt lump," the drever cried;
"Small stump," good Bloom replied;
"A little mite, to meäke so light,
  O' jolly Bloom the miller."

"You'd best be off now perty quick,"
    Cried Bloom, "an' vind a lighter lwoad,
Or else I'll vetch my voot, an' kick
    The vooty thing athirt the road."
"Who is the man?" they cried, "meäke room,"
"A halfstarv'd Do'set man," cried Bloom;
"You be?" another cried;
"Hee! Hee!" woone mwore replied.
"Aye, shrunk so thin, to bwone an' skin,"
  Cried worthy Bloom the miller.

AUNT'S TANTRUMS

Why ees, aunt Anne's a little staïd,
But kind an' merry, poor wold maïd!
If we don't cut her heart wi' slights,
She'll zit an' put our things to rights,
Upon a hard day's work, o' nights;
    But zet her up, she's jis' lik' vier,
      An' woe betide the woone that's nigh'er.
    When she is in her tantrums.

She'll toss her head, a-steppèn out
Such strides, an' fling the païls about;
An' slam the doors as she do goo,
An' kick the cat out wi' her shoe,
Enough to het her off in two.
    The bwoys do bundle out o' house,
      A-lassen they should get a towse,

When aunt is in her tantrums.
She whurr'd, woone day, the wooden bowl
In such a veag at my poor poll;
It brush'd the heäir above my crown,
An' whizz'd on down upon the groun',
An' knock'd the bantam cock right down;
    But up he sprung, a-teäkèn flight
    Wi' tothers, cluckèn in a fright,
      Vrom aunt in such a tantrum!

But Dick stole in, an' reach'd en down
The biggest blather to be voun',
An' crope an' put en out o' zight
Avore the vire, an' plimm'd en tight
An crack'd en wi' the slice there right.
    She scream'd, an' bundled out o' house,
    An' got so quiet as a mouse,—
      It frightened off her tantrum.

OUT A-NUTTÈN

Last week, when we'd a haul'd the crops,
We went a-nuttèn out in copse,
Wi' nuttèn-bags to bring hwome vull,
An' beaky nuttèn-crooks to pull
The bushes down; an' all o's wore
Wold clothes that wer in rags avore,
An' look'd, as we did skip an' zing,
Lik' merry gipsies in a string,
    A gwaïn a-nuttèn.

Zoo drough the stubble, over rudge
An' vurrow, we begun to trudge;
An' Sal an' Nan agreed to pick
Along wi' me, an' Poll wi' Dick;
An' they went where the wold wood, high
An' thick, did meet an' hide the sky;
But we thought we mid vind zome good
Ripe nuts among the shorter wood,
    The best vor nuttèn.

We voun' zome bushes that did feäce
The downcast zunlight's highest pleäce,
Where clusters hung so ripe an' brown,
That some slipp'd shell an' vell to groun'.
But Sal wi' me zoo hitch'd her lag
In brembles, that she coulden wag;
While Poll kept clwose to Dick, an' stole
The nuts vrom's hinder pocket-hole,
    While he did nutty.

An' Nanny thought she zaw a sneäke,
An' jump'd off into zome girt breäke,
An' tore the bag where she'd a-put
Her sheäre, an' shatter'd ev'ry nut.
An' out in vield we all zot roun'
A white-stemm'd woak upon the groun',
Where yollor evenèn light did strik'
Drough yollow leaves, that still wer thick
    In time o' nuttèn,

An' twold ov all the luck we had
Among the bushes, good an' bad!
Till all the maïdens left the bwoys,
An' skipp'd about the leäze all woys
Vor musherooms, to car back zome,
A treat vor father in at hwome.
Zoo off we trudg'd wi' clothes in slents
An' libbets, jis' lik' Jack-o'-lents,
    Vrom copse a-nuttèn.

LYDLINCH BELLS

When skies wer peäle wi' twinklèn stars,
An' whislèn aïr a-risèn keen;
An' birds did leäve the icy bars
To vind, in woods, their mossy screen;
When vrozen grass, so white's a sheet,
Did scrunchy sharp below our veet,

An' water, that did sparkle red
At zunzet, wer a-vrozen dead;
The ringers then did spend an hour
A-ringèn changes up in tow'r;
Vor Lydlinch bells be good vor sound,
An' liked by all the naïghbours round.

An' while along the leafless boughs
O' ruslèn hedges, win's did pass,
An' orts ov haÿ, a-left by cows,
Did russle on the vrozen grass,
An' maïdens' païls, wi' all their work
A-done, did hang upon their vurk,
An' they, avore the fleämèn brand,
Did teäke their needle-work in hand,
The men did cheer their heart an hour
A-ringèn changes up in tow'r;
Vor Lydlinch bells be good vor sound,
An' liked by all the naïghbours round.

There sons did pull the bells that rung
Their mothers' weddèn peals avore,
The while their fathers led em young
An' blushèn vrom the churches door,
An' still did cheem, wi' happy sound,
As time did bring the Zundays round,
An' call em to the holy pleäce
Vor heav'nly gifts o' peace an' greäce;
An' vo'k did come, a-streamèn slow
Along below the trees in row,
While they, in merry peals, did sound
The bells vor all the naïghbours round.

An' when the bells, wi' changèn peal,
Did smite their own vo'ks window-peänes,
Their sof'en'd sound did often steal
Wi' west winds drough the Bagber leänes;
Or, as the win' did shift, mid goo
Where woody Stock do nessle lew,

Or where the risèn moon did light
The walls o' Thornhill on the height;
An' zoo, whatever time mid bring
To meäke their vive clear vaïces zing,
Still Lydlinch bells wer good vor sound,
An' liked by all the naïghbours round.

THE ZILVER-WEED

The zilver-weed upon the green,
    Out where my sons an' daughters plaÿ'd,
Had never time to bloom between
    The litty steps o' bwoy an' maïd.
But rwose-trees down along the wall,
    That then wer all the maïden's ceäre,
An' all a-trimm'd an' traïn'd, did bear
    Their bloomèn buds vrom Spring to Fall.

But now the zilver leaves do show
    To zummer day their goolden crown,
Wi' noo swift shoe-zoles' litty blow,
    In merry plaÿ to beät em down.
An' where vor years zome busy hand
    Did traïn the rwoses wide an' high;
Now woone by woone the trees do die,
    An' vew of all the row do stand.

THE WIFE A-LOST

Since I noo mwore do zee your feäce,
    Up steäirs or down below,
I'll zit me in the lwonesome pleäce,
    Where flat-bough'd beech do grow:
Below the beeches' bough, my love,
    Where you did never come,
An' I don't look to meet ye now,
    As I do look at hwome.

Since you noo mwore be at my zide,
    In walks in zummer het,
I'll goo alwone where mist do ride,
    Drough trees a-drippèn wet:
Below the raïn-wet bough, my love,
    Where you did never come,
An' I don't grieve to miss ye now,
    As I do grieve at home.

Since now bezide my dinner-bwoard
    Your vaïce do never sound,
I'll eat the bit I can avword,
    A-vield upon the ground;
Below the darksome bough, my love,
    Where you did never dine,
An' I don't grieve to miss ye now,
    As I at hwome do pine.

Since I do miss your vaïce an' feäce
    In praÿer at eventide,
I'll praÿ wi' woone sad vaïce vor greäce
    To goo where you do bide;
Above the tree an' bough, my love,
    Where you be gone avore,
An' be a-waïtèn vor me now,
    To come vor evermwore.

STARTING IN LIFE

A windy evening, deep in June,
Was losing sunlight for the moon,
And towards my house the grass blades leant,
And towards my house the treeboughs bent;
And houseward all the pond waves sped,
And then the smoke to eastward spread
As I came home, and at my side
Brought in my newly-wedded bride,
Where first, by my pale light, was seen
In her new place the place's queen.

There I, the while the sun's last light
Beshaded things of every hight,
Was proud to see my grass for hay,
And proud to see my own trees sway,
And proud to see my own waves run,
And smoke upcurl from my own tun;
But proud was I with higher pride
To see, within her house, my bride,
And give her over for her own
What heretofore I held alone.

A mare had I, of easy pace,
And footsure, with a whitestarr'd face,
That trode my grass with roaming feet
And sought my tree from burning heat,
And drank beside the pool's wide bed,
And laid within my stall her head;
And she would come, at call, to bear
Her mistress both with speed and care,
To town, or on her homeward track
To pitch on toetip from her back.

When short-day'd winter came around,
And evening soon bedimm'd the ground,
And all the grass was white with frost,
And leaves of trees were dead and lost,
And shining ice bespread the pool,
And curling smoke upfloated cool,
My blazing fire flung back the gloom
Of night fast gath'ring o'er my room,
And show'd in kindly smiles a sight
Well worth the costliest of light.

THE DUET

As late at a house I made my call,
A mother and daughter's voices rang,
In two treble songs, they sweetly sang,
Strain upon strain, and fall by fall.

The mother was comely, still, but staid,
The daughter was young, but womantall,
As people come on, to great from small,
Maid upon child, and wife upon maid.

And oh! where the mother, in the train
Of years, may have left her child alone,
With no fellow voice to match her own,
Song upon song, and strain by strain,

May Providence show the way to bring
Her voice to be mine; with me to stay,
While softly my life may wear away,
Summer by summer, spring by spring.

ARISE, O WINDS!

Arise, O winds, and drive away
    The curling fog by mound or nook,
For we to-day would see you play
    Along the lightly-sparkling brook.
        By brook and brake,
        O winds, awake.

Arise! but do not mar our way
    With clouds of dust to blind our eyes,
For we would look this holiday
    On all the charms of land and skies.
        By hill and lake,
        O winds, awake.

O winds, blow on! but do not fly
    With dark'ning clouds of sudden show'rs,
For we would pass the fields all dry
    Among the heads of summer flow'rs.
        Sweep hill and plain,
        But not with rain.

And come to-night to clear away
  The clouds that o'er the moon may pass,
For we may wish to see you play
  By moonshades on the beech-side grass.
    So make, we pray,
    A happy day.

THE ORCHARD

Within the orchard's many shadows,
  Flitting softly round our feet,
While burning hot, the sunlight shot
  Between them in the summer heat;
We went, at times, by dock-leaves, falling
Limp, beside the mossy walling.

The way from garden into orchard
  Through an archèd gateway led,
Where rose a dovecote up above
  The grey old arch, above the head,
By flower-beds of the oldest fashion,
Sweet with rose and red carnation.

There spreading trees of mossy oldness,
  This and that way leaning lay;
And others, young and upright, sprung
  For year-stunn'd old ones cast away;
Within a thorny hedge that girded
Ground, and tree bough, many birded.

There shone the boughs, in May's gay sunshine,
  Out in blooth as white's a sheet;
Or else their flowers fell in showers
  Softly down about their feet;
Or else they nodded, many-appled,
Green, or lastly ruddy-dappled.

And then the time of apple-taking
  Came, and apples pattered down
Below the trees in twos and threes,
  Full thick; and yellow, red, and brown,
To folks that filled, from baskets by them,
Bags as full as they could tie them.

3. 'Without a drift'

E.M. Forster described Barnes as a 'yes man' (Forster 1951). The comment has frequently been thought a criticism, meaning that Barnes offered a view of society that accepted its bleaker and more disturbing aspects through omitting them from his poems. However, Bernard Jones recalls Forster explaining to him that the phrase was not pejorative but instead implied that Barnes's attitude to life was positive and affirmative: he said 'yes' to life through the beautiful images and contented, constructive personae of his poems. It is true, however, that Barnes claimed to have written only one poem with a 'drift' (Scott 1887: 323). The poem he referred to was the original version of his eclogue, 'The Times' (PWB I: 226). On its first publication, in the Dorset County Chronicle in 1838, the poem was called 'The Unioners' and contained the name of a local man, the Rev. Octavius Piers, who warned labourers against the dangers of civil war. The reference to Piers had gone by the time the poem appeared in Barnes's 1844 collection, so it seems that for Barnes a 'drift' meant a contentious political angle. Nevertheless, even without the name of Piers, the eclogue is still political, if conservatively so. It advises caution on the part of those who would demand, by force if necessary, a vote and a change of government: 'The men that you mid trust / To help you, Tom, would help their own zelves vu'st' [...] 'You'll meäke things wo'se, i'-ma'-be, by a riot.' (PWB I: 226, ll. 39-40, 222). Moreover, a political perspective, though cautious and conservative, is evident not only in this eclogue but across the range of Barnes's poems, and it is one which is rooted in a concern for the agricultural poor.

Barnes's own experience of landwork came from his childhood. His grandfather had been a yeoman farmer and his father a tenant farmer. However, his father encountered financial difficulties and a farming uncle was bankrupted. Barnes watched the disintegration of his uncle's farm and wrote in *Views of Labour and Gold* (1859), his book on political and moral economy, of the family's distress as the cows and the hay-making wagon were taken away. Ever afterwards he remembered his uncle's satisfaction in reaping the rewards of hard work from land in which he had some measure of ownership, and valued the happy freedom he had experienced at the farm, playing with his cousins. Freedom and a degree of independence — though within a hierarchy and combined with hard work — are praised throughout Barnes's writing. In this respect he had something in common with a number of contemporary political and economic thinkers.

But although, in poems like 'My Orcha'd in Linden Lea' (PWB I: 233), Barnes celebrated independence and freedom and abhorred the control of a 'peevish' employer, he admired the philanthropic local squire with 'kindly words upon his tongue, / Vor he did know the poor so well / 'S the richest vo'k in Culver Dell' ('Culver Dell and the Squire': PWB I: 273). And when common land was enclosed, depriving poor families of the opportunity to keep livestock on it and add to their income, he applauded the squire, 'a worthy man, / That vu'st brought into ouer pleäce the plan' to rent out allotments. These allotments would provide opportunities not only to supplement family incomes but also for young boys, as they watched their elders at work, to 'learn the vaster / The way to do things when they have a meäster'. Moreover,

> ...the work do keep em out o' harm;
> Vor vo'ks that don't do nothèn wull be vound
> Soon doèn woorse than nothèn, I'll be bound.
> ('The 'Lotments': PWB I: 93)

Work, in Barnes's view, was vital. He shared Carlyle's belief, expressed in *Past and Present* (1844), in its nobleness and sacredness. Poll, a milk-maid in one of his poems, is as happy 'As if she wore a goolden crown' and 'Noo leädy, wi' her muff an vaïl, / Do walk wi' sich a steätely tread', ('The Milk-maïd o' the Farm'; PWB I: 80). The community he respects does not grow up 'peäle an' weak' because it works

> ....wi' health an' strength,
> Vrom mornèn drough the whole day's length,
> An' sleep do come wi' the dew.
> ('Sleep did come wi' the Dew'; PWB I: 106)

The fruits of this labour would benefit the community as well as the individual. 'Our Fathers' Works' admires the hedges, trees and buildings left behind by previous generations and urges:

> Zoo now mid nwone ov us vorget
> The pattern our vorefathers zet;
> But each be faïn to underteäke

Some work to meäke vor others' gaïn,
That we mid leäve mwore good to sheäre,
Less ills to bear, less souls to grieve,
   (PWB I: 270)

However, Barnes did not approve of every kind of labour. He was opposed
to the kind of specialisation which prevented workers from carrying out
a task in its entirety. Instead he admired the resourceful self-sufficiency of
the labourer who, as in 'Work an' Wait' (PWB I: 547), forms bricks from
clay and thatch from dried grass to construct a home for his bride.

This kind of self-reliance was a contemporary theme — expressed,
for example, in Samuel Smiles' *Self Help* (1859) — and was at the centre
of Barnes's own life, in the self-education he began as a very young man
and in his contribution to the development of adult education. He also
regretted, as in the eclogue, 'Two Farms in Woone' (PWB I: 160), the
denial of advancement to labourers through the practice of combining
smallholdings into farms.

Nevertheless, Barnes did not wish to encourage advancement merely
for the sake of material gain. In *Views of Labour and Gold* he was critical
of a concentration on work which denied families the opportunity of 'purer'
forms of pleasure. And in 'The Leäne' he feared that

...wealth is wo'th now mwore than health is wo'th;
  Let it al goo,
If 't 'ull bring but a sov'rèn or two.
   (PWB I: 306)

In this respect Barnes resembled Ruskin who wrote in *Unto this Last* (1862)
that life's capacity for love and joy is true wealth. Though Ruskin was a
major influence on the first Labour M.P.s, he began his autobiography
claiming to be a Tory. Barnes was also traditionally conservative in his
acceptance of the social hierarchy, but his emphasis on duty to the community
and his abhorrence of money-making for its own sake come close, suggests
the historian Chris Wrigley, to Christian socialism (Wrigley 1984: 11-12).

These views of hard work, for the self and for others, resonate
throughout Barnes's life. He did not write with an aggressive 'drift': he
did not protest against anything in his poems. Nonetheless, as his son
Miles contended, he showed a 'passive courage' (Hinchy 1966: 66). That
courage is displayed in his poetry's quiet but determined advocacy, despite
the century's changing ways, of the kind of rural life that he remembered
from childhood, a life he believed essential for the health, self-respect and
moral welfare of the individual and the community.

ECLOGUE: THE 'LOTMENTS

John and Richard

JOHN

Zoo you be in your groun' then, I do zee,
A-workèn and a-zingèn lik' a bee.
How do it answer? what d'ye think about it ?
D'ye think 'tis better wi' it than without it ?
A-recknèn rent, an' time, an' zeed to stock it,
D'ye think that you be any thing in pocket?

RICHARD

O', 'tis a goodish help to woone, I'm sure o't.
If I had not a-got it, my poor bwones
Would now ha' eäch'd a-crackèn stwones
Upon the road; I wish I had zome mwore o't.

JOHN

I wish the girt woones had a-got the greäce
To let out land lik' this in ouer pleäce;
But I do fear there'll never be nwone vor us,
An' I can't tell whatever we shall do:
We be a'mwost starvèn, an' we'd goo
To 'merica, if we'd enough to car us.

RICHARD

Why 'twer the squire, good now! a worthy man,
That vu'st brought into ouer pleäce the plan;
He zaid he'd let a vew odd eäcres
O' land to us poor leäb'rèn men;
An', faith, he had enough o' teäkers
Vor that, an' twice so much ageän.
Zoo I took zome here, near my hovel,
To exercise my speäde an' shovel;
An' what wi' dungèn, diggèn up, an' zeedèn,
A-thinnèn, cleänèn, howèn up an' weedèn,
I, an' the biggest o' the childern too,
Do always vind some useful jobs to do.

JOHN

Aye, wi' a bit o' ground, if woone got any,
Woone's bwoys can soon get out an' eärn a penny;
An' then, by workèn, they do learn the vaster
The way to do things when they have a meäster;
Vor woone must know a deäl about the land
Bevore woone's fit to lend a useful hand,
In geärden or a-vield upon a farm.

RICHARD

An' then the work do keep em out o' harm;
Vor vo'ks that don't do nothèn wull be vound
Soon doèn woorse than nothèn, I'll be bound.
But as vor me, d'ye zee, with theäse here bit
O' land, why I have ev'ry thing a'mwost:
Vor I can fatten vowels for the spit,
Or zell a good fat goose or two to rwoast;
An' have my beäns or cabbage, greens or grass,
Or bit o' wheat, or, sich my happy feäte is,
That I can keep a little cow, or ass,
An' a vew pigs to eat the little teäties.

JOHN

An' when your pig's a-fatted pretty well
Wi' teäties, or wi' barley an' some bran,
Why you've a-got zome vlitches vor to zell,
Or hang in chimney-corner, if you can.

RICHARD

Aye, that's the thing; an' when the pig do die
We got a lot ov offal for to fry,
An' netlèns for to bwoil; or put the blood in,
An' meäke a meal or two o' good black-pudden.

JOHN

I'd keep myzelf from parish, I'd be bound,
If I could get a little patch o' ground.

CULVER DELL AND THE SQUIRE

There's noo pleäce I do like so well,
As Elem Knap in Culver Dell,
Where timber trees, wi' lofty shouds,
Did rise avore the western clouds;
An' stan' ageän, wi' veathery tops,
A-swayèn up in North-Hill Copse.
An' on the east the mornèn broke
Above a dewy grove o' woak:
An' noontide shed its burnèn light
On ashes on the southern height;
An' I could vind zome teäles to tell,
O' former days in Culver Dell.

An' all the vo'k did love so well
The good wold squire o' Culver Dell,
That used to ramble drough the sheädes
O' timber, or the burnèn gleädes,
An' come at evenèn up the leäze
Wi' red-eär'd dogs bezide his knees.
An' hold his gun, a-hangèn drough
His eärmpit, out above his tooe,
Wi' kindly words upon his tongue,
Vor vo'k that met en, wold an' young,
Vor he did know the poor so well
'S the richest vo'k in Culver Dell.

An' while the woak, wi' spreadèn head,
Did sheäde the foxes verny bed;
An' runnèn heäres, in zunny gleädes,
Did beät the grasses' quiv'rèn' bleädes;
An' speckled pa'tridges took flight
In stubble vields a-feädèn white;
Or he could zee the pheasant strut
In sheädy woods, wi' päinted cwoat;
Or long-tongued dogs did love to run
Among the leaves, bezide his gun;
We didden want vor call to dwell
At hwome in peace in Culver Dell.

But now I hope his kindly feäce
Is gone to vind a better pleäce;
But still, wi' vo'k a-left behind
He'll always be a-kept in mind,
Vor all his springy-vooted hounds
Ha' done o' trottèn round his grounds,
An' we have all a-left the spot,
To teäke, a-scatter'd, each his lot;
An' even Father, lik' the rest,
Ha' left our long vorseäken nest;
An' we should vind it sad to dwell,
Ageän at hwome in Culver Dell.

The aïry mornèns still mid smite
Our windows wi' their rwosy light,
An' high-zunn'd noons mid dry the dew
On growèn groun' below our shoe;
The blushèn evenèn still mid dye,
Wi' viry red, the western sky;
The zunny spring-time's quicknèn power
Mid come to open leaf an' flower;
An' days an' tides mid bring us on
Woone pleasure when another's gone.
But we must bid a long farewell
To days an' tides in Culver Dell.

THE MILK-MAÏD O' THE FARM

O Poll's the milk-maïd o' the farm!
    An' Poll's so happy out in groun',
Wi' her white païl below her eärm
    As if she wore a goolden crown.

An' Poll don't zit up half the night,
    Nor lie vor half the day a-bed;
An' zoo her eyes be sparklèn bright,
    An' zoo her cheäks be bloomèn red.

In zummer mornèns, when the lark
    Do rouse the litty lad an' lass
To work, then she's the vu'st to mark
    Her steps along the dewy grass.

An' in the evenèn, when the zun
    Do sheen ageän the western brows
O' hills, where bubblèn brooks do run,
    There she do zing bezide her cows.

An' ev'ry cow of hers do stand,
    An' never overzet her païl;
Nor try to kick her nimble hand,
    Nor switch her wi' her heavy taïl.

Noo leädy, wi' her muff an' vaïl,
    Do walk wi' sich a steätely tread
As she do, wi' her milkèn païl
    A-balanc'd on her comely head.

An' she, at mornèn an' at night,
    Do skim the yellow cream, an' mwold
An' wring her cheeses red an' white,
    An' zee the butter vetch'd an' roll'd.

An' in the barken or the ground,
    The chaps do always do their best
To milk the vu'st their own cows round,
    An' then help her to milk the rest.

Zoo Poll's the milk-maïd o' the farm!
    An' Poll's so happy out in groun',
Wi' her white païl below her eärm,
    As if she wore a goolden crown.

OUR FATHERS' WORKS

Ah! I do think, as I do tread
Theäse path, wi' elems overhead,
A-climèn slowly up vrom Bridge,
By easy steps, to Broadwoak Ridge,
That all theäse roads that we do bruise
Wi' hosses' shoes, or heavy lwoads;
An' hedges' bands, where trees in row
Do rise an' grow aroun' the lands,
Be works that we've a-vound a-wrought
By our vorefathers' ceäre an' thought.

They clear'd the groun' vor grass to teäke
The pleäce that bore the bremble breäke,
An' draïn'd the fen, where water spread,
A-lyèn dead, a beäne to men;
An' built the mill, where still the wheel
Do grind our meal, below the hill;
An' turn'd the bridge, wi' arch a-spread,
Below a road, vor us to tread.

They vound a pleäce, where we mid seek
The gifts o' greäce vrom week to week;
An' built wi' stwone, upon the hill,
A tow'r we still do call our own;
With bells to use, an' meäke rejaïce,
Wi' giant vaïce, at our good news:
An' lifted stwones an' beams to keep
The raïn an' cwold vrom us asleep.

Zoo now mid nwone ov us vorget
The pattern our vorefathers zet;
But each be faïn to underteäke
Some work to meäke vor others' gaïn,
That we mid leäve mwore good to sheäre,
Less ills to bear, less souls to grieve,
An' when our hands do vall to rest,
It mid be vrom a work a-blest.

LIFE

A-field, from day to day,
　　We see quick shapes of life at ev'ry turn,
Each seeking, in its way,
　　The forms of good for which its kind may yearn.
But oh! the ways
　　Of might with helplessness, where life is strife,
And oh! the woes
　　Of smaller, slain to yield the stronger life.

We see the hare's last springs
　　Of fear-strain'd limbs, before the harrier's feet;
We see the sparrow's wings
　　Flap out, below the hawk, their dying beat.
Where pools may lie
　　The swallow sweeps away the dancing fly;
In streamlets low,
　　To yield the pike more life, the perch must die.

But then, again, we see
　　The faithful bird o'erwatch his sitting hen,
And watch-rooks on the tree
　　To warn the grounded flock of coming men.
In loving mood
　　Stand horses, neck o'er neck, within the cool;
And down the mead
　　The cows, all friendly, seek the drinking pool.

And what, then, must we deem
　　That our best good is built on others' ill?
Or may it rather seem
　　That we are blest in lovingness of will?
Howe'er it be,
　　All we are bidden to be kind to all,
As days come by,
　　And still enhance the good of great and small.

FELLOWSHIP

Well here, another year, at least,
We go along with blinking sight,
By smoky dust arising white
Up off our road, to Lincham feast.
With trudging steps of tramping feet,
We souls on foot, with foot-folk meet:
For we that cannot hope to ride
For ease or pride, have fellowship.

And so, good father tried to show
To folk, with hands on right or left
Down-pull'd by some great bundle's heft,
And trudging weary, to or fro,
That rich men are but one to ten
When reckon'd off with working men,
And so have less, the while the poor
Have ten times more of fellowship.

He thought, good man, whatever part
We have to play, we all shall find
That fellowship of kind with kind
Must keep us better up in heart;
And why should working folk be shy
Of work, with mostly work-folk by,
While kings must live in lonesome states,
With none for mates in fellowship?

Tall chimneys up with high-flown larks,
And houses, roods in length, with sights
Of windows, glaring off in lights
That shoot up slopes of wood-bound parks,
Are far and wide, and not so thick
As poor men's little homes of brick,
By ones or twos, or else in row
So small and low, in fellowship.

But we, wherever we may come,
Have fellowship in hands and loads,
And fellowship of feet on roads;
And lowliness of house and home;
And fellowship in homely fare,
And homely garb for daily wear;
And so may Heaven bless the more
The working poor in fellowship.

4. Circles of Language

Barnes became a distinguished linguist. By the middle of his life he had learnt at least sixty languages, had described the Dorset Blackmoor Vale dialect in a 'Dissertation' (first published with his *Poems of Rural Life in the Dorset Dialect:* Barnes 1844), and had developed theories of language which are explained in a variety of articles and books, including *A Philological Grammar* (1854).

These theories involved a notion of linguistic purity. To Barnes, a language could be called 'pure' if it is clearly descended from what he called its 'roots' or 'primitives'. He believed that such essential roots could be found by tracing each language back to its origins. He had faith in origins because he believed in the unsurpassed goodness of God's original creation of all things — including, in his view, languages. Consequently he deeply regretted what he took to be a deterioration of the English language, a loss of its original 'purity', through the addition of Latin, Greek and French modifications. The word '*port-feuille*' could not, he argued in his article 'Corruptions of the English Language' (1830), express to an Englishman the function of the article better than the word 'papercase'. 'Papercase' is an example of the creation from English 'roots' that he preferred to borrowing from other languages. He wrote:

> If we take 1 for the noun-root, 2 for the adjective-root, 3 for the verb-root, 4 for an adverb, and 5 for a preposition, we may form a set of handy expressions for the formation of compound words:(Barnes 1854: 70)

> [and we] enrich and purify our speech by the inbringing of words of forms already known and received. Of the verb-form (2+en) we may take 'greaten' (instead of the borrowed to *exaggerate*); of the noun-form (5-1) we may take 'foredraught', a *programme*; and of the adjective form (3+some) we may have 'bendsome' for *flexible*. (Barnes 1832: 269).

This process is, of course, a conscious employment of the kind of morphological rules followed, with less awareness, in everyday use of language. For example, Barnes has generated the verb 'to greaten' in the way that, without thinking, English speakers produce the verb 'to whiten' from the adjective 'white' plus the morpheme 'en'.

Some of this theory and practice found its way into Barnes's schoolroom, for he believed that Standard English, with its borrowings, had become a language 'fit only for learned people to converse with each other in, being no longer one in which the more learned can easily teach the less so' (Barnes 1830: 501). Its traces can also be found in his poetry. 'The Old Oak' (PWB II: 875), for instance, describes people 'upcrouching' within a hollow trunk, and 'A Rock-room' (PWB II: 848) talks of its speaker safe in 'hidelock' within a 'rock-room' of strong rock walls and thick stone roof. 'The Stonen Steps' (PWB II: 879) writes of movements that are 'childquick' or 'womanslow'. Moreover, Barnes's preference for originality no doubt fostered the creation of lovely and apt compounds in phrases like 'cheäk-burnèn seasons o' mowèn', 'hot-slippered veet' and 'worold-hushen night' ('Childhood', 'Fatherhood', 'Vields in the Light'; PWB I: 259, 256, 101).

Barnes's belief in linguistic purity also encouraged his use of the local dialect. He thought it likely that Dorset speech was descended from a different Anglo-Saxon dialect than Standard English. The latter, he implies in his Dissertation, originated with the Angles of Slesvig. But he believed that 'Dorsetshire fell under the power of the West Saxons, and received their language, the venerable parent of its present rustic dialect' (Barnes 1844: Dissertation para 10). This language had been protected from later foreign additions because the area was surrounded by woods and hills. Its purity could only have been relative, however. Even Barnes's Blackmoor dialect speakers would have been familiar with the word 'beef', yet it is of Norman origin and not Anglo-Saxon: 'sugar' is a descendant of Sanskrit: 'tea' is Chinese.

Nevertheless, Barnes's theory of purity was linked to a belief in the specialness of each language and language variety. He approved of the Arabic proverb, 'a man by learning a second language becomes two', which suggests that a language both forms and expresses a person's identity. This implication has something in common with the conviction of Wihelm von Humboldt — a nineteenth century philologist whose ideas Barnes would surely have encountered in his linguistic studies — that 'each language draws a magic circle round the people to which it belongs, a circle from which there is no escape save by stepping out of it into another' (Cassirer

1946: 9). In order to allow his pupils the opportunity to step within the circles of different cultures, Barnes taught them languages. Over the years his curriculum offered Latin, Greek, Anglo-Saxon, French, German, Danish, Italian, Portuguese, Spanish, Swedish, Hebrew and Hindustani. Moreover, by writing in the Blackmoor dialect Barnes not only represented the local identity: he also allowed readers from outside the community an opportunity to step within its circle.

Of course, writing in dialect was hardly new. Spenser incorporated local speech forms in his 'Shepherds' Calendar'; some of Shakespeare's characters, like the Welsh Fluellen, had spoken with a suggestion of English varieties. But, in the late eighteenth and the nineteenth century, suggestions and approximations of dialects became more precise with, for instance, the work of Robert Burns, George Eliot, the Brontës and Tennyson. Such precision was no doubt encouraged by the Victorian interest in philology, fostered by German and British work in comparative Indo-European linguistics. But an increased focus on dialects was also a reaction to the industrial development that was fracturing communities and fostering new urban Englishes. And it was a response to education that disseminated a Standard form of speech. W.A. Wright called in 1870 for the immediate foundation of a dialect society to record and preserve local forms of English, insisting that 'In a few years it will be too late. Railroads and certificated teachers are doing their work' (Wright 1870: 271). Thomas Hardy's Tess d'Urberville bears fictional testimony to the fact, for she had been introduced to Standard English in her rural Wessex village by a London-trained school mistress.

Nevertheless, the resistance to Non-Standard language that has been powerful in the twentieth century was also experienced by nineteenth century dialect writers, including Barnes. When the *Hampshire Advertiser* published an example of Barnes's dialect poetry it noted 'we cannot so far prefer our native "Doric", to what we must with all deference call good English, as to give more than one specimen' (Barnes's papers in the Dorset County Museum: Vol 1, p. 46). However, when Barnes read his dialect poems aloud in Dorchester Town Hall, local audiences, Barnes's daughter Lucy Baxter recalled, were delighted to hear their 'daily life portrayed in [their] own common speech' (Scott 1887: 167).

This enthusiastic local testimony would suggest that, although literary renderings of dialect would again become more impressionistic later in the nineteenth century (probably because these were less taxing for Standard-speaking readers), Barnes's use of the Blackmoor dialect was generally accurate. It would be surprising had it not been, given his linguistic skill and apparent conviction that local language is an index of local identity. He certainly used the 'expressive features' peculiar to the Blackmoor variety and he admired its 'broad and bold shape...rich in humour, strong in raillery and hyperbole' for this, he believed, made it altogether a fit 'vehicle of rustic feeling and thought' (Barnes 1844: Dissertation para 11).

One of these 'expressive features' is the adjective ending 'some'. Barnes discusses it in more detail in his article 'On English Derivatives' (1831) where he argues that 'some' means strictly 'apt to do' or 'promote' the thing denoted, whereas 'ful' means 'having much of a thing'. Thus, in Barnes's view, 'delightful', spoken of music, is incorrect, whilst 'delightsome' is acceptable on the grounds that 'music cannot have, or be full of, delight itself, but is apt to delight a man, or to promote delight in his mind'. He uses this formation in the following lines from 'Fair Emily of Yarrow Mill'.

An aïr o' zumer nights do blow
  Athirt the vields in playsome flight,
'Tis then delightsome under all
The sheädes o' boughs by path or wall,
  (PWB I, 265)

Evidently 'playsome' has been chosen here, instead of 'playful', because whilst flight cannot be full of anything, the breeze in its flight may be 'apt to play' with the grass in its path.

A further defining feature of the dialect is the use of 'he'. Barnes writes:

> The masculine pronoun *he* or *'e* is still used in Dorset for inanimate nouns, as *he* was in Anglo-Saxon; in which language, as a consequence of its case-endings, many things without life were taken as of the masculine or feminine gender. Indeed it is sometimes said in joke that every thing is *he* but a tom cat, and that is *she*. (Barnes 1844: Dissertation para 43)

There is nothing self-consciously literary, then, when in 'Leädy-Day, an' Riddèn House' (PWB I: 73) Barnes writes, of the frying pan, that eggs 'slide /In butter round his hissèn zide'.

A further Non-standard use of pronouns, the choice of 'I' or 'he' as object where Standard English speakers would select 'me' or 'him', is explained by Barnes as a deliberate substitution for emphasis (1844: Dissertation para. 46). Unemphatically, a Dorset speaker would say 'Gi'e *me* the pick'. But emphatically he would prefer 'Gi'e the pick to *I, not he*', using nominatives rather than accusatives and achieving emphasis by giving equal syntactic prominence to both agent and recipient.

> An' if dost think that thou canst challenge I
> At any thing, — then, Bob, we'll teäke a pick a-piece...
> ('Eclogue: The Best Man in the Vield'; PWB I: 117)

Barnes also explained in his Dissertation (para 54) the Dorset use of the auxiliary 'did'. A Dorset verb was conjugated with the auxiliary when it was intended to denote a continuous or repeated action. Thus, a Dorset speaker distinguished 'He walked to work' (on that day) from 'He did walk to work' (every day). The auxiliary is a persistent feature in the dialect poems, contributing to a sense of past security and permanence. The sun 'did' shine, the birds 'did' sing, the people 'did' meet for work or play, throughout the day, and day after day.

> A-boomèn deep, did slowly sound
>   The bell, a-tellèn middle night;
> The while, the quiv'rèn ivy, round
>   The tree, did sheäke in softest light.
> ('Moonlight on the Door'; PWB I: 366)

Obviously it is syntactic features such as these which make the Dorset variety Non-standard. There are also marked differences between the vocabularies of Standard English and Barnes's dialect. Yet it may not always be apparent to Standard speakers that they are hearing a word that does not belong to their own English variety. It will be clear, of course, that the Standard user needs to discover that for nineteenth century Dorset speakers 'widdicks' meant small brushwood and that 'drong' has two possible meanings, a narrow way or a throng of people, whilst to 'coleplexy' was to 'glean the few apples left on the tree after intaking'. (Fortunately Barnes provides a helpful glossary after a number of his collections, including those of 1844 and 1879). But it may not always be obvious to the Standard hearer of the poems that some words mean different things in the two varieties. Take, for instance, 'Sound o' Water' (PWB I: 311). This dialect poem will be completely misunderstood by the Standard reader if 'lawn' is assumed to carry its Standard meaning, something like (as it is defined in an edition of the Penguin English dictionary) 'a stretch of flat ground covered with close-mown grass'.

I born in town! oh no, my dawn
O' life broke here beside theäse lawn;

To Barnes and local readers, the word would have signified, according to
the glossary in Bernard Jones's 1962 edition of the poems, the 'unploughed
part of a field'. It is therefore an appropriate choice of word to emphasise
the free and unfettered nature of the speaker's rural birthplace by contrast
with the town which he goes on to describe as claustrophobic and stressful.

Many of Barnes's basically Standard English poems on local rural themes
also include Blackmoor words within them, like 'leaze', 'clote', 'bennet'
(unmown field, water-lily, flower-stalks of grass). Presumably these remained
for Barnes the best signifiers of objects or concepts whose meanings he
associated firmly with their local contexts. He remarks in his Dissertation
that Dorset speech has distinctive words which Standard English can only
distinguish by periphrasis and he writes in his Standard English poems of
winds 'huffling', of sleet or falling apples 'happering' (bouncing up from
the ground) and of cows that are 'cappled' (white muzzled).

However, not only are there hints of Dorset grammar and vocabulary
in Barnes's Standard writing. The orthography of the dialect work makes
clear that the pronunciation of these poems is local and significantly
different from Standard speech. Nevertheless, as the section, 'A "mellow"
tone' explains, there are still similarities of sound between Barnes's Standard
and Non-standard poems. But none of these resemblances between the
two 'circles' of language are surprising. Although Barnes claimed to be
writing poems 'of their own' for local people in local language, this language
was the dialect he spoke from a child, and the life it reveals was the life
he lived as a child. The Non-standard poems therefore speak out as much
for Barnes himself as for the local labouring families, whilst the Standard
poems inevitably bear traces of the Blackmoor circle of life and language
that he continued to love into old age. In this sense, all of Barnes's poems,
whatever their variety of English, are personally speaking.

LEÄDY-DAY AN' RIDDÈN HOUSE

Aye, back at Leädy-Day, you know,
I come vrom Gullybrook to Stowe;
At Leädy-Day I took my pack
O' rottletraps, an' turn'd my back
Upon the weather-beäten door,
That had a-screen'd, so long avore,
The mwost that theäse zide o' the greäve,
I'd live to have, or die to seäve!
My childern, an' my vier-pleäce,
Where Molly wi' her cheerful feäce,
When I'd a-trod my wat'ry road
Vrom night-bedarken'd vields abrode,
Wi' nimble hands, at evenèn, blest
Wi' vire an' vood my hard-won rest;
The while the little woones did clim',
So sleek-skinn'd, up from lim' to lim',
Till, strugglèn hard an' clingèn tight,
They reach'd at last my feäce's height,
All tryèn which could soonest hold
My mind wi' little teäles they twold.
An' riddèn house is such a caddle,
I shan't be over keen vor mwore o't,
Not yet a while, you mid be sure o't,—
I'd rather keep to woone wold staddle.

Well, zoo, avore the east begun
To redden wi' the comèn zun,
We left the beds our mossy thatch
Wer never mwore to overstratch,
An' borrow'd uncle's wold hoss *Dragon*,
To bring the slowly lumbrèn waggon,
An' when he come, we vell a-packèn
The bedsteads, wi' their rwopes an' zackèn;
An' then put up the wold eärm-chair,
An' cwoffer vull ov e'then-ware,
An' vier-dogs, an' copper kittle,
Wi' crocks an' saucepans, big an' little;
An' fryèn-pan, vor aggs to slide

In butter round his hissèn zide,
An' gridire's even bars, to bear
The drippèn steäke above the gleäre
O' brightly-glowèn coals. An' then,
All up o' top o' them ageän
The woaken bwoard, where we did eat
Our croust o' bread or bit o' meat,—
An' when the bwoard wer up, we tied
Upon the reäves, along the zide,
The woaken stools, his glossy meätes,
Bwoth when he's beäre, or when the pleätes
Do clatter loud wi' knives, below
Our merry feäces in a row.
An' put between his lags, turn'd up'ard,
The zalt-box an' the corner cupb'ard.
An' then we laid the wold clock-ceäse,
All dumb, athirt upon his feäce,
Vor we'd a-left, I needen tell ye,
Noo works 'ithin his head or belly.
An' then we put upon the pack
The settle, flat upon his back;
An' after that, a-tied in pairs
In woone another, all the chairs,
An' bits o' lumber wo'th a ride,
An' at the very top a-tied,
The childern's little stools did lie,
Wi' lags a-turn'd toward the sky:
Zoo there we lwoaded up our scroff,
An' tied it vast, an' started off.
An',—as the waggon cooden car all
We had to teäke,—the butter-barrel
An' cheese-wring, wi' his twinèn screw,
An' all the païls an' veäts, an' blue
Wold milk leads, and a vew things mwore,
Wer all a-carr'd the day avore.
And when the mwost ov our wold stuff
Wer brought outside o' thik brown ruf,
I rambled roun' wi' narrow looks,
In fusty holes an' darksome nooks,
To gather all I still mid vind,

O' rags or sticks a-left behind.
An' there the unlatch'd doors did creak,
A-swung by winds, a-streamèn weak
Drough empty rooms, an' meäkèn sad
My heart, where me'th woonce meäde me glad.
Vor when a man do leäve the he'th
An' ruf where vu'st he drew his breath,
Or where he had his bwoyhood's fun,
An' things wer woonce a-zaid an' done
That took his mind, do touch his heart
A little bit, I'll answer vor't.
Zoo riddèn house is such a caddle,
That I would rather keep my staddle.

GRAMMER'S SHOES

I do seem to zee Grammer as she did use
Vor to show us, at Chris'mas, her weddèn shoes,
An' her flat spreadèn bonnet so big an' roun'
As a girt pewter dish a-turn'd upside down;
    When we all did draw near
    In a cluster to hear
O' the merry wold soul how she did use
To walk an' to dance wi' her high-heel shoes.

She'd a gown wi' girt flowers lik' hollyhocks,
An' zome stockèns o' gramfer's a-knit wi' clocks,
An' a token she kept under lock an' key, —
A small lock ov his heäir off avore 't wer grey.
    An' her eyes wer red,
    An' she shook her head,
When we'd all a-look'd at it, an' she did use
To lock it away wi' her weddèn shoes.

She could tell us such teäles about heavy snows,
An' o' raïns an' o' floods when the waters rose
All up into the housen, an' carr'd awoy
All the bridge wi' a man an' his little bwoy;

An' o' vog an' vrost,
An' o' vo'k a-lost,
An' o' peärties at Chris'mas, when she did use
Vor to walk hwome wi' gramfer in high-heel shoes.

Ev'ry Chris'mas she lik'd vor the bells to ring,
An' to have in the zingers to heär em zing
The wold carols she heärd many years a-gone,
While she warm'd em zome cider avore the bron';
    An' she'd look an' smile
    At our dancèn, while
She did tell how her friends now a-gone did use
To reely wi' her in their high-heel shoes.

Ah! an' how she did like vor to deck wi' red
Holly-berries the window an' wold clock's head,
An' the clavy wi' boughs o' some bright green leaves,
An' to meäke twoäst an' eäle upon Chris'mas eves;
    But she's now, drough greäce,
    In a better pleäce,
Though we'll never vorget her, poor soul, nor lose
Gramfer's token ov heäir, nor her weddèn shoes.

SOUND O' WATER

I born in town! oh no, my dawn
O' life broke here beside theäse lawn;
Not where pent aïr do roll along,
In darkness drough the wall-bound drong,
An' never bring the goo-coo's zong,
Nor sweets o' blossoms in the hedge,
Or bendèn rush, or sheenèn zedge,
    Or sounds o' flowèn water.

The aïr that I've a-breath'd did sheäke
The draps o' raïn upon the breäke,
An' bear aloft the swingèn lark,
An' huffle roun' the elem's bark,

In boughy grove, an' woody park,
An' brought us down the dewy dells,
The high-wound zongs o' nightengeäles,
    An' sounds o' flowèn water.

An' when the zun, wi' vi'ry rim,
'S a-zinkèn low, an' wearèn dim,
Here I, a-most too tired to stand,
Do leäve my work that's under hand
In pathless wood or oben land,
To rest 'ithin my thatchèn oves,
Wi' ruslèn win's in leafy groves,
    An' sounds o' flowèn water.

THISSLEDOWN

The thissle down by winds a-roll'd
    In Fall along the zunny plaïn,
Did catch the grass, but lose its hold,
    Or cling to bennets, but in vaïn.

But when it zwept along the grass,
    An' zunk below the hollow's edge,
It lay at rest while winds did pass
    Above the pit-bescreenèn ledge.

The plaïn ha' brightness wi' his strife,
    The pit is only dark at best,
There's pleasure in a worksome life,
    An' sloth is tiresome wi' its rest.

Zoo, then, I'd sooner beär my peärt,
    Ov all the trials vo'k do rue,
Than have a deadness o' the heart,
    Wi' nothèn mwore to veel or do.

THE OLD OAK

O grey-knotted oak, with ribbèd trunk,
    That, hollowed by time, art now a shell,
Where we in our early days have sunk,
    Upcrouching within thy wooden cell;
As there for a-while we linger'd dry,
From storm-driven rain that scudded by.

How gay is the path along thy ledge
    When daisies besprinkle all the ground,
And thorns are in bloom along the hedge
    Where lately the woodpecker has found
A bower within her doorway, high
In thee, as the rook is sweeping by.

At night on the moon-shown path below
    Thy head only men-folk take their way,
Where women by choice would only show
    Their comelier shapes while shines the day;
And not when thy broken moonshades lie
Where swiftly the meal-white owl sweeps by.

When flakes of grey moss that thou has shed
    In storms are all dried by summer heat,
And footweary men beneath thy head
    Would willingly sit to rest their feet,
Then happy, the while the sun is high,
Is he who beholds my love come by.

THE STORM

The raving storm is rife, and where a beam
    Of sunlight pierces through the misty cloud,
The spreading waters of the river gleam
    Below the ruff'ling wind that roars aloud
      Among the writhing saplings, lowly bow'd
With wildly fitful fury, till they seem
To sweep the ground, while trickling waters stream
    Adown their green-ribb'd sides. The cattle crowd

Before the weatherbeaten hedge, and man
    Below some roof that rocks above his head
      Seeks shelter from the heavy rolling blast:

And twitt'ring birds all shield them where they can,
    Below the dripping tree or broad-eav'd shed,
      Until the fury of the storm is past.

CHANGE OF HOMES

Ah! Rosy, I know, was ever fond
    Of Linchy-cliff Mill, her childhood's home,
Where still through the mill's broadshining pond
    The mill-race rolls on with hissing foam;
And still up above the hatches float
The leaves of the summer's yellow clote;
And ever, as rolls the water-wheel,
The fast-whirling millstones shed their meal;
And oft the strong team pull on the wain,
Well laden with grain, beside the stream.

And Jenny's kind heart would ever cling
    To Tway-knap farmhouse's mossy wall,
Where leazes were flow'ry through the spring,
    And gold-yellow corn reel'd ripe in fall.
There oft she had seen, in harvest heat,
Arise the wide-bulging ricks of wheat,
And known every cow with wide horned head,
Or cappled, or starr'd, or sleeky red;
And seen the men fill with sacks of grain
The well-rolling wain, to go to mill.

And Jane of the farm at length became
    The bride of the son that took the mills;
And Rose of the mills took up the name
    That Jane had cast off at Tway-knap hills.
And each of the two for ever felt
Strong love for the home where erst she dwelt,

And each for the other kindly cared,
And asked how her old home's friends all fared
Whenever the wain came in at mill
Or up at the hill came home again.

But while at each happy home sweet life
    Ran peacefully fair, at length each bride
Was smitten by sore disease then rife
    In summertide's tainted air, and died;
And, though of earth's homes they had the best,
Were called to new homes by far more blest,
And nevermore asked, with kindly care,
How all at their early homes might fare
Whenever the wain came in at mill
Or up on the hill came home again.

5. 'Closeness of phrase to his vision'

Thomas Hardy, writing in the introduction to his collection of Barnes's poems, approved his friend's skill in achieving 'a closeness of phrase to his vision' (Hardy 1908: viii). This accomplishment may be illustrated through a comparison between some of Barnes's original Dorset dialect poems and his translation of these into Standard English. For the translations, in attempting to maintain metrical and rhyme schemes in a variety of English that has, by definition, a number of different features from the version first chosen, frequently lose some of the effectiveness — the closeness of phrase to vision — of the originals. Indeed, it is odd that Barnes made such translations, for he himself believed that 'the spirit of the author always evaporates in the process of translation' (Barnes's papers in the Dorset County Museum: Vol. 21, p. 34).

Geoffrey Grigson disagreed, at least as far as Barnes is concerned, maintaining that 'Barnes does translate, and without a great loss' (Grigson 1950: 12). He offered as proof the lines,

> The gookoo over white-weäv'd seas
> Do come to zing in thy green trees.

arguing that these lose nothing when he converts them to

> The cuckoo over white-waved seas
> Do come to sing in thy green trees.

Yet the Standard version obviously sacrifices those linguistic features, peculiar to the Blackmoor dialect, which identify the original lines and their speaker as representative of a particular community and culture. More than this, losing a diaeresis — the separate pronunciation, indicated by the marker (¨) of two adjacent vowels — and replacing a voiced /z/ with unvoiced /s/ alters the length and resonance of the lines. These are tiny phonetic alterations and the difference they make is slight. But their removal could change an image that carries hints of movement and significant sound (as 'A "mellow" tone' argues) into a bland statement of fact.

Other pairs of poems, translated by Barnes, suffer not only through phonetic alteration but also through syntactic and lexical change. Take, for example, the dialect first version of 'The Wind at the Door' (PWB I: 565) and its Standard translation (PWB II: 844). The former poem names the beloved: Jeäne. The Standard version refers instead to 'my love'. The change did not need to be made in order to preserve a rhyme or metrical scheme in the translation. But many of the dialect poems call the much-loved woman they describe 'Jeäne', and Barnes's daughter, Lucy, believed (Scott 1887: 122-123) they frequently referred to her mother, Julia. 'The Wind at the Door' — in its original form, at any rate — certainly seems to relate to Julia Barnes, for it is about loss and longing, and Barnes was deeply affected by his beloved wife's death. But the poem in translation concerns a more stereotypical, seemingly shallower woman than the original version's personality. Perhaps, then, Barnes was reluctant to distinguish her in this Standard version by the name he had frequently attached to poetic memories of his much loved Julia.

The translation also lacks immediacy as a result of changes that, unlike the alteration from proper noun to common noun, are needed to preserve the original's form. The poignant 'I zot me sad' of the dialect version cannot be matched in the syntax of Standard English. And once Standard 'sitting' has been selected, the remaining syllables of the line must also change to maintain metre. In the process, reference to the speaker's emotional state is lost and 'eventide' becomes 'voiceless evening'. No doubt 'voiceless' is suggested by the 'dumb', silent house. But the word has a literary formality entirely lacking from the original poem. Also, a sense of deep and personal feeling is conveyed more poignantly in the first line of the dialect's last stanza than it is in the translation for, whilst the subject of the original is 'I', the translation displaces the person with the abstract noun phrase, 'my fond illusion'. Something of the sort has to happen because whilst 'broke' must be kept for the rhyme, the syllable of its prefix 'a-' must be replaced for the Standard.

The more stereotypical image of a woman in the translation is also encouraged by syntactically-related lexical change which is necessitated in order to maintain the poem's form. 'Noo soul a-steppèn' must be altered because 'a-' has to go. 'Fair one', so different in its meaning from 'soul', makes up the missing syllable. 'Stepping' could have remained, but the pretty image of 'fair one' is perhaps better developed by 'tripping': tripping could certainly not have followed soul.

Yet all this is not to say that Barnes could not write well in Standard English, with equal closeness of phrase to vision. Poems whose first versions were in the Standard variety are generally as effective as those that originated in the dialect.

It is true that Barnes was not particularly successful in his earliest Standard English attempts, poems that he wrote in his late teens which are rather mannered, their diction somewhat conventional. Take, for example, the second stanza from 'Lines: Addressed to an Oak near my Father's Cottage'.

> Oft have I sat in thy expansive head,
>   A fancied monarch of the space below;
> Oft on thy trunk my youthful cheek I've laid,
>   Wet with the tears I shed for fancied woe.
> (PWB I: 29)

Nevertheless, a technique of precise observation came to the fore when Barnes chose to direct his work away from inner thoughts and towards the people and objects of his surroundings. There are small hints of this even in the early Standard poems. For example, 'Destiny' seems to have been inspired by a humorous look at Barnes's courtship with the woman, Julia Miles, who would eventually become his wife. The selection of a few simple details, to sketch a clear image of a gipsy's appearance and manner, is a foretaste of the descriptive technique he will develop in his later work.

> 'Twas a gipsy proceeding fatigu'd to the tent
>   That was pitch'd in a neighbouring nook,
> And her gait was inclin'd and her strength was nigh spent,
> For under the weight of two infants she bent,
> And hobbling, and grumbling, and poking she went,
>   Nor behind or before deign'd to look.
> (PWB I: 25)

Then, when Barnes began writing in dialect about local places, people and events, his poems became unpretentious, his language vivid and precise.

The later Standard poems, written after the first poems in dialect, are comparably clear and evocative. The following is the second stanza of 'The Storm-wind'. Its simple vocabulary produces a perfect snapshot of the effort to stay upright in a storm, as well as the effect of the wind on the landscape.

The man that is staggering by
 Holds his hat to his head by the brim;
And the girl, as her hair-locks outfly,
 Puts a foot out, to keep herself trim,
And the quivering wavelings o'erspread
The small pool where the bird dips his head.
 (PWB II: 832)

Barnes's poems, in both Standard and Non-standard English, are full of such images, people caught in moments of doing and being. Hardy compared them to Dutch art, 'brief and unaffected, but realistic as a Dutch painting' (Hardy 1879: 470). Barnes himself admired the Dutch school for its 'beauty and truth of colour and action' (Barnes 1861: 137). Certainly the animals of his poems are active.There is the 'stiff-snouted swine, that would plough / Up the soft-bladed grass' ('Home', PWB II: 805), and the bull that is 'blaring / And tearing the ground' ('On the Hill' PWB II: 756), and rabbits that 'out ov wood at veed, / At zight o' men do scote all back' ('The Surprise', PWB II: 567). And the people do not merely observe: they participate in local life and they experience its landscape. So it is that instructions to a loved one, to do this and do that in order to keep warm, are integrated with the image in 'Wind Screens' of a weather-beaten night.

And wear not your shoes too thin to tread
 The dead leaves on the danky ground,
 Nor under the wind-flung twigs go round
To-night with unhooded head;
And muffle your shoulders warm
From blasts of the wind now stormy.
 (PWB II: 832)

In another poem, though Uncle and Aunt's appearance is described through their clothes — 'His hat wer broad, his cwoat wer brown, / Wi' two long flaps a-hangèn down' — these two come closer into vision through details of their behaviour:

...aunt did pull her gown-taïl drough
Her pocket-hole, to keep en neat,

An' then aunt zaid 'twer time to goo
In hwome, — a-holdèn up her shoe,
To show how wet he wer wi' dew.
    ('Uncle an' Aunt'; PWB I: 108; stanzas 2, 6)

The landscape too is often brought to the mind's eye not merely by
description of its elements but by reference to their effect on the people
of the community. In winter, for instance, 'the vield's 'a-vroze so white'
that it is

Too hard tonight to spweil your clothes.
You got noo pools to waddle drough,
Nor clay a-pullèn off your shoe.
    ('The Vrost'; Barnes PWB I: 162)

The relationship between the land and the people was important to
Barnes. As 'Our Fathers' Works' (PWB I: 270) explains, he was convinced
that each man contributes something to the landscape through his work.
A man's legacy — perhaps in the form of a building, a road he worked
on, a hedge he planted — will remain to enrich the lives of future
generations and also to remind them of their ancestry. Moreover, the
present landscape and its events are a constant reminder of personal history.
For example, the blackbird's 'evenen-whissle' recalls for an adult his
boyhood's search for a nest, climbing

...aloft, wi' clingèn knees,
Vor crows' aggs up in swaÿèn trees,
While frighten'd blackbirds down below
Did chatter o' their little foe.
    ('The Blackbird'; Barnes PWB I: 78)

Barnes's images are generally, like this one, precisely spatio-temporally
located, particularly through the deixis (indication of context and
relationship to context) of the adverbs *there, then, where and when,* and of
the past tense. Together these aspects of language give a strong sense of
times and places past and of their relationship to the present. The poems
point, from the here and now, to locations, objects, events and people
that were once important and that continue to exist through present
memory. This happens, for example, in 'Zummer Stream' in the beginning
of its first stanza:

Ah! then the grassy-meäded Maÿ
Did warm the passèn year, an' gleam
Upon the yollow-grounded stream,
That still by beech-tree sheädes do straÿ.

and in its second stanza:

There by the path, in grass knee-high,
Wer buttervlees in giddy flight,
All white above the deäisies white,
Or blue below the deep blue sky.

This, like many other Barnes poems, acknowledges and welcomes the presence of a younger generation, now living in a place which invites memory, so that past and present unite.

'Tis good to come back to the pleäce,
   Back to the time, to goo noo mwore;
'Tis good to meet the younger feäce
   A-mentèn others here avore.
As streams do glide by green mead-grass,
My zummer-brighten'd years do pass.
   (PWB I: 402)

However, this new generation rarely looks forward. An anxiety which prevents all but the most tentative glance at its future is bred of a recognition, made plain throught Barnes's work, that the present is a period of transition to — in his view — a harsher world. It is a recognition that is clear in the images and deixis of 'Times o' Year'. The following lines are extracts from this poem, taking the reader from past to present and on to contemplate an uncertain future.

Here did swaÿ the eltrot flow'rs,
When the hours o' night wer vew,

There the milkmaïd hung her brow
By the cow, a-sheenèn red;

Now the cwolder-blowèn blast,
Here do cast vrom elems' heads

Soon shall grass, a-vrosted bright,
Glisten white instead o' green,
An' the wind shall smite the cows,
Where the boughs be now their screen.
Things do change as years do vlee;
What ha' years in store vor me?
  (PWB I: 414; lines from stanzas 1, 2, 3, 4)

The precision of place and time that is marked in poems like this one
contributes to the literalness of their vision. Barnes rarely used symbolism
to express his perceptions of life and land. Occasionally he chose a simile,
commenting, for example, that the wind can sometimes blow a stream
back against its downward flow,

As man, while hope beguiles him, thinks
His life is rising, while it sinks.
  ('The Wind up the Stream'; PWB II: 823)

Metaphor, however, is relatively rare and never complex, maybe because
Barnes's respect for the accuracy of languages confined him to the literal
and inhibited his innovation.

It is perhaps in consequence of this restriction that Barnes's thinking,
in his poems, is not complex. He claimed simply to write the pictures that
he saw in his mind. But the language that he chose creates these pictures
with a profound and evocative beauty and precision. To return to the
comparison between his work and Dutch painting, the art historian,
Gombrich, writes that Vermeer's seventeenth century paintings have a

strange and unique combination of mellowness and precision ... They
make us see the quiet beauty of a simple scene with fresh eyes and
give us an idea of what the artist felt when he watched the light
flooding through the window and heightened the colour [within a
room]. (Gombrich 1978: 340)

Though written about painting, this paragraph might well apply to Barnes,
given his personal conviction (discussed in 'A "mellow" tone') that local
people and the language they used were both mellow. Moreover, there is
always light in his poems, heightening and mellowing images as in a
Vermeer. Barnes liked May-time most of all, because it has a 'sparklèn'

'brightness' which means the butterflies can 'gleäm the mwost by [its] gaÿ light' ('May'; PWB I: 20). Indeed, gleaming colour is an ever-present feature of his work, seen not only in the brilliance of butterfly wings but also in yellow gil-cups, white hedge-row blossoms, red waggon wheels, purple berries, the dog's coal-black nose and russet ear.

A considerable number of Barnes's modifiers are, however, not merely adjectives of colour. They include expressive compounds, as in 'the moon-climb'd height o' the sky' ('My Love's Guardian Angel'; PWB I: 367) and 'the storm-be-smother'd bell' ('The Flood in Spring'; PWB I: 381). Some of his contemporaries were critical of similar phrases on the grounds that they were unlikely to have been spoken by the poems' field-working personae. But Hardy, in his 1908 collection of the poems, defends their use on the grounds of artistic precision and beauty. Certainly Barnes's chosen language expressed a vision and atmosphere authentic enough for Gerard Manley Hopkins to comment that 'Dorset life and landscape had taken flesh and tongue' through the images of the poems (Abbott 1938: 220-222).

THE WIND AT THE DOOR [I]

As day did darken on the dewless grass,
    There still, wi' nwone a-come by me,
    To staÿ awhile at hwome by me,
    Within the house, all dumb by me,
I zot me sad as evenèntide did pass.

An' there a win'-blast shook the rattlèn door,
    An' seem'd, as win' did mwoan without,
    As if my Jeäne, alwone without,
    A-stannèn on the stwone without,
Wer there a-come wi' happiness oonce mwore.

I went to door; an' out vrom trees above
    My head, upon the blast by me,
    Sweet blossoms wer a-cast by me,
    As if my love, a-past by me,
Did fling em down—a token ov her love.

"Sweet blossoms o' the tree where I do murn,"
    I thought, "if you did blow vor her,
    Vor apples that should grow vor her,
    A-vallèn down below vor her,
O then how happy I should zee you kern."

But no. Too soon I voun' my charm a-broke.
    Noo comely soul in white like her—
    Noo soul a-steppèn light like her—
    An' nwone o' comely height like her—
Went by; but all my grief ageän awoke.

THE WIND AT THE DOOR [II]

As daylight darken'd on the dewless grass,
    There still, with no one come by me,
    To stay awhile at home by me,
    Within the house, now dumb by me,
I sitting let the voiceless evening pass.

And there a windblast shook the rattling door,
And sounded in a moan without,
As if my love, alone without,
And standing on the stone without,
Had there come back with happiness once more.

I went to door, and out from trees above
My head, upon the blast by me,
Sweet blossoms there were cast by me,
As if my love had pass'd by me,
And flung them down, a token of her love.

Sweet blossoms of the tree where now I mourn,
I thought, if you could blow for her,
For apples that should grow for her,
And fall red-ripe below for her,
O then how happy I should see you kern.

But no. Too soon my fond illusion broke.
No comely soul in white like her—
No fair one tripping light like her—
No wife of comely height like her—
Went by; but all my grief again awoke.

CLOUDS [I]

A-ridèn slow, at lofty height,
    Wer clouds, a-blown along the sky,
O' purple-blue, an' pink, an' white,
    In pack an' pile, a-reachèn high,
A-shiftèn off, as they did goo,
    Their sheäpes vrom new ageän to new.

An zome like rocks an' tow'rs o' stwone,
    Or hills or woods, a-reachèn wide;
An' zome like roads, wi' doust a-blown,
    A-glitt'rèn white up off their zide,
A-comèn bright, ageän to feäde
    In sheäpes a-meäde to be unmeäde.

Zoo things do come, but never stand,
    In life. It mid be smiles or tears,
A jaÿ in hope, an' one in hand,
    Zome grounds o' grief, an' zome o' fears;
It mid be good, or mid be ill,
    But never long a-standèn still.

CLOUDS [II]

Onriding slow, at lofty height,
Were clouds in drift along the sky,
Of purple-blue, and pink, and white,
In pack and pile, upreaching high,
For ever changing, as they flew,
Their shapes from new again to new.

And some like rocks and towers of stone,
Or hills or woods, outreaching wide;
And some like roads, with dust upblown
In glittering whiteness off their side,
Outshining white, again to fade
In figures made to be unmade.

So things may meet, but never stand,
In life. They may be smiles or tears,
A joy in hope, and one in hand,
Some grounds of grief, and some of fears;
They may be good, or may be ill,
But never long abiding still.

THE BLACKBIRD

Ov all the birds upon the wing
Between the zunny show'rs o' spring, —
Vor all the lark, a-swingèn high,
Mid zing below a cloudless sky,

An' sparrows, clust'rèn roun' the bough,
Mid chatter to the men at plough,—
The blackbird, whisslèn in among
The boughs, do zing the gaÿest zong.

Vor we do hear the blackbird zing
His sweetest ditties in the spring,
When nippèn win's noo mwore do blow
Vrom northern skies, wi' sleet or snow,
But dreve light doust along between
The leäne-zide hedges, thick an green;
An' zoo the blackbird in among
The boughs do zing the gaÿest zong.

'Tis blithe, wi' newly-open'd eyes,
To zee the mornèn's ruddy skies;
Or, out a-haulèn frith or lops
Vrom new-plesh'd hedge or new-vell'd copse,
To rest at noon in primrwose beds
Below the white-bark'd woak-trees' heads;
But there's noo time, the whole day long,
Lik' evenèn wi' the blackbird's zong.

Vor when my work is all a-done
Avore the zettèn o' the zun,
Then blushèn Jeäne do walk along
The hedge to meet me in the drong,
An' staÿ till all is dim an' dark
Bezides the ashen tree's white bark;
An' all bezides the blackbird's shrill
An' runnèn evenèn-whissle's still.

An' there in bwoyhood I did rove
Wi' pryèn eyes along the drove
To vind the nest the blackbird meäde
O' grass-stalks in the high bough's sheäde:
Or clim' aloft, wi clingèn knees,
Vor crows' aggs up in swaÿen trees,

While frighten'd blackbirds down below
Did chatter o' their little foe.
An' zoo there's noo pleäce lik' the drong,
Where I do hear the blackbird's zong.

EVENÈN IN THE VILLAGE

Now the light o' the west is a-turn'd to gloom,
    An' the men be at hwome vrom ground;
An' the bells be a-zendèn all down the Coombe
    From tower, their mwoansome sound.
      An' the wind is still,
      An' the house-dogs do bark,
An' the rooks be a-vled to the elems high an' dark,
    An' the water do roar at mill.

An' the flickerèn light drough the window-peäne
    Vrom the candle's dull fleäme do shoot,
An' young Jemmy the smith is a-gone down leäne,
    A-plaÿèn his shrill-vaïced flute.
      An' the miller's man
      Do zit down at his ease
On the seat that is under the cluster o' trees,
    Wi' his pipe an' his cider can.

MEÄPLE LEAVES BE YOLLOW

Come, let's stroll down so vur's the poun',
Avore the sparklèn zun is down:
The zummer's gone, an' days so feäir
As theäse be now a-gettèn reäre.
The night, wi' mwore than daylight's sheäre
    O' wat'ry sky, do wet wi' dew
    The ee-grass up above woone's shoe,
      An' meäple leaves be yollow.

The last hot doust, above the road,
An' vu'st dead leaves ha' been a-blow'd
By plaÿsome win's where spring did spread
The blossoms that the zummer shed;
An' near blue sloos an' conkers red
 The evenèn zun, a zettèn soon,
  Do leave a-quiv'rèn to the moon,
   The meäple leaves so yollow.

Zoo come along, an' let's injaÿ
The last fine weather while do staÿ;
While thou canst hang, wi' ribbons slack,
Thy bonnet down upon thy back,
Avore the winter, cwold an' black,
 Do kill thy flowers, an' avore
  Thy bird-cage is a-took in door,
   Though meäple leaves be yollow.

BEAUTY UNDECKED

The grass mid sheen when wat'ry beäds
O' dew do glitter on the meäds,
An' thorns be bright when quiv'rèn studs
O' raïn do hang upon their buds—
As jewels be a-meäde by art
To zet the plaïnest vo'k off smart.

But sheäkèn ivy on its tree,
An' low-bough'd laurel at our knee,
Be bright all day, without the gleäre,
O' drops that duller leaves mid wear—
As Jeäne is feäir to look upon
In plaïnest gear that she can don.

BROWN BENNETS

With the acorns yet green on the wide-spreading oak,
    While the grass was yet green in his shade,
That had holden it cool from the sun's burning stroke
    As it brown'd all the hill and the glade;
There the wind of the fall, in a blast
Flitted fast, o'er the dry-headed bennets.

With folk that, on Sunday, then tripp'd o'er the ground
    To the grey-tower'd church on the height,
There the sound of the bells' mellow chiming was drown'd
    By the bough-sweeping wind in its flight,
As it made the white thistle-down fly
Low and high, by the brown-headed bennets.

And from hence, on a workday, by gateways and stiles,
    And by brook-brim and elm-shaded bank,
We all merrily wended o'er quick-trodden miles
    On the pathways, that climb'd or that sank,
To the fair under Hambledon's side,
Sinking wide, with the brown-headed bennets.

There the close-thronging people, the great with the small,
    Were all streaming about on the ground,
Like the pool-filling water that, under its fall,
    Will keep giddily wallowing round,
Where to-day all the down is left bare
To the air-blast that shakes the brown bennets.

And dear are the paths of their quick-tripping feet
    Out by Manston and Sturminster tow'rs,
And the high-shooting maypole in Shillingston street
    For the may-dance, with spring-quickened flow'rs;
Or Hammoon, or by Ockford, with wide-reaching ground,
Green, or brown'd with the dry-headed bennets.

THE BENCH BY THE GARDEN WALL

As day might cool, and in the pool
The shaded waves might ripple dim,
We used to walk, or sit in talk,
Below the limetree's leaning limb,
Where willows' drooping boughs might fall
Around us, near the garden wall.

Where children's heads on evening beds,
In dull-ear'd sleep, were settled sound,
The moon's bright ring would slowly spring
From down behind the woody mound,
With light that slanted down on all
The willows nigh the garden wall.

By roof-eaves spread up over head,
There clung the wren's brown nest of hay,
In wind to make the ivy shake,
And your dark locks of hair to play,
As there you told the news of all
The day, beside the garden wall.

The while the sun had far to run,
On high, above the green-tree'd land,
Few days would come for jaunts from home,
And none without some work on hand,
Yet we enjoy'd at eveningfall
Our bench beside the garden wall.

Our flowers blew, our fruit well grew,
To hang in air, or lie on ground;
Our bees would hum, or go and come,
By small-door'd hives, well hackled round.
All this we had, and over all
Our bench beside the garden wall.

6. A 'mellow' tone

In a 'Dissertation on the Dorset Dialect of the English Language' (which first appeared the 1844 collection, *Poems of Rural Life in the Dorset Dialect* and was extended in its second edition) Barnes wrote that the Blackmoor variety of English had 'a mellowness which is sometimes wanting in the national speech' (Barnes 1844: Dissertation para 62). By mellowness he seems to have meant a softness of sound and a gentle ease of rhythm, for he thought the effect he had in mind was achieved partly by 'the elisions of harsh consonants', and partly by 'the frequent use of the syllabic augment *a* in participles of verbs' (Barnes 1844: Dissertation para 55). The following lines from 'The May-tree' support his view.

> I've a-come by the Maÿ-tree all times o' the year,
>   When leaves wer a-springèn,
>   When vrost wer a-stingèn,
> When cool-winded mornèn did show the hills clear,
> When night wer bedimmèn the vields vur an' near.
> (PWB: 301)

Here, the presence of the syllable 'a' separates consonants and thereby eases the transition from one to the other. In addition, pronouncing Standard final 'ing' syllables as 'èn', typical of the dialect, avoids a cluster which to some ears might sound hard and abrupt. Moreover, eliding the fricative /f/ in the line 'I've a-come by the Maÿ-tree all times o' the year' not only removes an arguably noisy-sounding consonant but in addition permits the rhythm to pulse steadily without interruption.

The pronunciation of both vowels in adjacent pairs, described in the Dissertation (Barnes 1844: paras 19, 21, 22, 24, 27), is another feature of the Blackmoor voice that contributes to Barnes's smoothly flowing lines. The double sound is occasionally marked in the poems by a circumflex ('nâisy rooks') or, more usually, by a diaeresis over the second of the vowels ('bleäde').

An' we've a trod the sheenèn bleäde
Ov eegrass in the zummer sheäde,
An' when the leäves begun to feäde
W'i zummer in the weäne, Jeäne;
('Jeäne'; PWB I: 213)

The dialect's syntax also plays a part in the suggestion of mellowness. Blackmore present tense verbs took the auxiliary 'da' or 'do', and the past has an imperfect version using the auxiliary 'did'. These auxiliaries, throughout the poems, provide unstressed syllables for the metres that Barnes manages in gently even pace within his complex versification (see 'The skill that conceals skill'). In 'The May-tree', 'did' plays its part in the dactylic feet of 'When cool-winded mornèn did show the hills clear' . In 'Lydlinch Bells', 'did' and 'do' contribute to lines of four iambic feet.

An' when the bells, wi' changèn peal,
Did smite their own vo'ks window-peänes,
Their sof'en'd sound did often steal
Wi' west winds drough the Bagber leänes;
Or, as the win' did shift, mid goo
Where woody Stock do nessle lew,
(PWB I: 302)

'Did', as Barnes pointed out in his Dissertation (para 54), implied continuous or repeated action in Blackmoor usage. It might therefore contribute to a sense of mellowness not only through its effect on rhythm but also through its contribution to meanings of secure certainty. It appears to do so in 'Lydlinch Bells', where its use helps to make clear that life events are reassuringly repeated, family by family and generation after generation.

There sons did pull the bells that rung
Their mothers' weddèn peals avore,
The while their fathers led em young
And blushèn vrom the churches door,.
(PWB I: 302)

Mellowness is also achieved in Barnes's dialect poems through their intonational contours. For when they fall and rise on successive strong beats, the result is a gently rocking movement, sometimes like an incantation, sometimes a soothing lullaby, always assured and assuring, as in the first four lines of 'Our Be'thpleäce'.

How dear's the door a latch do shut,
An' geärden that a hatch do shut,
Where vu'st our bloomèn cheäks ha' prest
The pillor ov our childhood's rest;
    (PWB I: 274)

Yet mellowness need not have been the natural and inevitable result of local language in conjunction with poetic features. On occasion, Barnes seems to have consciously adjusted his phonetic choices to achieve the mellowness he believed he heard in local voices. For example, in successive editions of *Poems of Rural Life in the Dorset Dialect* he made changes to 'The Spring' (PWB I: 71) that seem to increase the richness of his sounds. In the first edition (1844), the fifth and sixth lines of the poem read:

An' we can hear birds zing, and zee
Upon the boughs the buds o' spring'.

Yet in the collection's second edition (1847) the fifth line has become:

When birds da zing, an' we can zee'

This version may sound more softly undulating because the two occurrences of stressed /z/ are separated by an additional stress which, moreover, adds a second gentle glide, /w/. But finally, in the 1879 collection, 'da' is replaced with 'do' and it may be that a yet smoother flow was intended by this adjustment for, in a Glossary at the end of the volume, Barnes notes that '*o*, when not under a strain of voice, is...as *e* in the French *le'* (Barnes 1879: 461).

Barnes's tinkering with the sounds of his dialect poems in this manner is unsurprising. For he believed the potential for mellowness in the Blackmoor Vale dialect helped to make it 'a good vehicle for the more tender feelings, as well as for the broader humour of rural life' (Barnes 1844 Dissertation: para 62) and it is these aspects of Dorset life that he wished to highlight, perhaps even to enhance.

Extracts given already in this section would seem to exemplify 'tender feelings'. But Barnes did not make clear his definition of 'broader humour'. If he had comedy in mind he could not, given his own sensitive nature and his admiration for tender feelings, have meant 'broader' in the sense of coarse. Possibly the phrase implies something like a simpler, less aggressive humour. The dialect poem 'John Bloom In Lon'on', describing a Dorset miller's excursion to the Crystal Palace which is doomed when his huge girth prevents him fitting into a 'tidy little cab', supports this interpretation.

> "Who is the man?" they cried, "meäke room, "
> "A halfstarv'd Do'set man," cried Bloom;
> "You be?" another cried;
> "Hee! Hee!" woone mwore replied.
> "Aye, shrunk so thin, to bwone an' skin,"
> Cried worthy Bloom the miller.
> (PWB I: 473, lines from stanzas 7, 8, 9)

Bernard Jones explains that the poem's teasing ending reflected a contemporary response. Dorset landworkers frequently retaliated against the assumption that they were underfed by claiming that town workers were unhealthy specimens compared with themselves. A ping-pong battle of slogans - like 'halfstarved', 'bone and skin' – was then exchanged between the two sides.

But of course Barnes created voices other than the lightheartedly comic or the warmly loving and contented. Robert, in the eclogue 'Two Farms in Woone', despairing that machines have taken his work, insists

> They hadden need meäke poor men's leäbour less,
> Vor work a'ready is uncommon skeä'ce.
> (PWB I: 102)

There is nothing mellow here. The same dialect that made the rise and fall of rich sound in 'Lydlinch Bells' and 'Our Be'thpleäce' doggedly beats out a protest through iambic pentametres that are sometimes emphasised by plosives. Moreover, the plosives /k/ and /p/, being awkwardly adjacent, seem to fracture the first line quoted here.

Nevertheless, this relatively harsh effect is the exception in Barnes's generally mellow dialect poems. Besides, and most importantly, mellowness may also be detected in those he wrote in Standard English. Many of the Standard lines have gently undulating intonational curves and steady, easy rhythms like those of the dialect poems. Obviously this effect cannot have been achieved with the help of augmented syllables or auxiliary verbs. These are not features of Standard English. Nonetheless, words have been chosen whose evenly balanced syllables produce lines of rolling, regular rhythm. They do so in, for example, 'The Moor', with its four iambic feet.

Where yonder leaning hill-side roves
    With woody dippings, far around,
And many jutting brows, and coves,
    Of rugged cliffs, and slopy ground,
Beside the stream that slowly sinks
    With reaches tinted from the skies,
And stream-side meadows, lowly lies
The moor, with dikes and sedgy brinks.
    (PWB II: 782)

There is no elision or syllable 'a' to prevent consonant clusters in this extract. But even without these softening features, sound moves smoothly through the lines. It can do so partly because of enjambement within each couplet and partly because several words begin or end with a vowel, or semi-vowel like /y/, that divides consonants across word boundaries. There is no dialectal diaeresis of course (the pronunciation of both adjacent vowels, as in 'Jeäne'). On the other hand, stress falls on high vowels and thus gently emphasises and lengthens them. There is also the repetition of /s/ whose alliteration eases the flow of sound.

The consequence is an impression of mellowness that is at odds with the 'rugged' landscape sketched in lines 3 and 4. But the contrast is not inappropriate since it heralds images that are to come later in the poem. For it is the comfortable and comforting moor upon which Barnes concentrates as he goes on to describe its willow's shade, lowing cows, boys playing and men contentedly fishing.

So, was the tender and 'broadly humoured' nature that Barnes believed typical of the local community, and offered throughout his dialect poems, as much — or perhaps even more — a part of his own adult, Standard English-speaking personality? His biographers describe a humane, sensitive and uncomplicated man, gentle in his relationships with family, friends, school pupils and parishioners. And it is, of course, reasonable to suppose that Barnes shared the characteristics he thought prevalent in the local community, for he himself was a local man, born to the local language. But surely it is equally likely that his loving personality projected his own gentle attitudes on to the varied natures of people around him, a possibility that lends further support to the argument that even Barnes's dialect poems speak out not only for Dorset labouring families but, in addition, represented his own mind and feelings just as much as the poems he wrote in Standard English.

JEÄNE

We now mid hope vor better cheer,
My smilèn wife o' twice vive year.
Let others frown, if thou bist near
    Wi' hope upon thy brow, Jeäne;
Vor I vu'st lov'd thee when thy light
Young sheäpe vu'st grew to woman's height;
I loved thee near, an' out o' zight,
    An' I do love thee now, Jeäne.

An' we've a-trod the sheenèn bleäde
Ov eegrass in the zummer sheäde,
An' when the leaves begun to feäde
    Wi' zummer in the weäne, Jeäne;
An' we've a-wander'd drough the groun'
O' swaÿèn wheat a-turnèn brown,
An' we've a-stroll'd together roun'
    The brook an' drough the leäne, Jeane.

An' nwone but I can ever tell
Ov all thy tears that have a-vell
When trials meäde thy bosom zwell,
    An' nwone but thou o' mine, Jeäne;
An' now my heart, that heav'd wi' pride
Back then to have thee at my zide,
Do love thee mwore as years do slide,
    An' leäve them times behine, Jeäne.

THE LILAC

Dear lilac-tree, a-spreadèn wide
Thy purple blooth on ev'ry zide,
As if the hollow sky did shed
Its blue upon thy flow'ry head;
Oh! whether I mid sheäre wi' thee
Thy open aïr, my bloomèn tree,
Or zee thy blossoms vrom the gloom,
'Ithin my zunless workèn-room,

My heart do leäp, but leäp wi' sighs,
At zight o' thee avore my eyes,
Vor when thy grey-blue head do swaÿ
In cloudless light, 'tis Spring, 'tis Maÿ.

'Tis Spring, 'tis Maÿ, as Maÿ woonce shed
His glowèn light above thy head—
When thy green boughs, wi' bloomy tips,
Did sheäde my childern's laughèn lips;
A-screenèn vrom the noonday gleäre
Their rwosy cheäks an' glossy heäir;
The while their mother's needle sped,
Too quick vor zight, the snow-white thread,
Unless her han', wi' lovèn ceäre,
Did smooth their little heads o' heäir;
Or wi' a sheäke, tie up anew
Vor zome wild voot, a slippèn shoe;
An' I did leän bezide thy mound
Ageän the deäsy-dappled ground,
The while the woaken clock did tick
My hour o' rest away too quick,
An' call me off to work anew,
Wi' slowly-ringèn strokes, woone, two.

Zoo let me zee noo darksome cloud
Bedim to-day thy flow'ry sh'oud,
But let en bloom on ev'ry spraÿ,
Drough all the days o' zunny Maÿ.

HALLOWED PLEÄCES

At Woodcombe farm, wi' ground an' tree
Hallow'd by times o' youthvul glee,
At Chris'mas time I spent a night
Wi' feäces dearest to my zight;
An' took my wife to tread, woonce mwore,
Her maïden hwome's vorseäken vloor,
An' under stars that slowly wheel'd
Aloft, above the keen-aïr'd vield,

While night bedimm'd the rus'lèn copse,
An' darken'd all the ridges' tops,
The hall, a-hung wi' holly, rung
Wi' many a tongue o' wold an' young.

There, on the he'th's well-hetted ground,
Hallow'd by times o' zittèn round,
The brimvul mug o' cider stood
An' hiss'd avore the bleäzèn wood;
An' zome, a-zittèn knee by knee,
Did tell their teäles wi' hearty glee,
An' others gamboll'd in a roar
O' laughter on the stwonen vloor;
An' while the moss o' winter-tide
Clung chilly roun' the house's zide,
The hall, a-hung wi' holly, rung
Wi' many a tongue o' wold an' young.

There, on the pworches bench o' stwone,
Hallow'd by times o' youthvul fun,
We laugh'd an' sigh'd to think o' neämes
That rung there woonce, in evenèn geämes:
An' while the swaÿèn cypress bow'd,
In chilly wind, his darksome sh'oud,
An' honeyzuckles, beäre o' leäves,
Still reach'd the window-sheädèn eaves
Up where the clematis did trim
The stwonen arches mossy rim,
The hall, a-hung wi' holly, rung
Wi' many a tongue o' wold an' young.

There, in the geärden's wall-bound square,
Hallow'd by times o' strollèn there,
The winter wind, a-hufflèn loud,
Did swaÿ the pear-tree's leafless sh'oud,
An' beät the bush that woonce did bear
The damask rwose vor Jenny's heäir;
An' there the walk o' peävèn stwone
That burn'd below the zummer zun,

Struck icy-cwold drough shoes a-wore
By maïdens vrom the hetted vloor
In hall, a-hung wi' holm, where rung
Vull many a tongue o' wold an' young.

There at the geäte that woonce wer blue
Hallow'd by times o' passèn drough,
Light strawmotes rose in flaggèn flight,
A-floated by the winds o' night,
Where leafy ivy-stems did crawl
In moonlight on the windblown wall,
An' merry maïdens' vaïces vled
In echoes sh'ill, vrom wall to shed,
As shiv'rèn in their frocks o' white
They come to bid us there " Good night,"
Vrom hall, a-hung wi' holm, that rung
Wi' many a tongue o' wold an' young.

There in the narrow leäne an' drong
Hallow'd by times o' gwaïn along,
The lofty ashes' leafless sh'ouds
Rose dark avore the clear-edged clouds,
The while the moon, at girtest height,
Bespread the pooly brook wi' light,
An' as our child, in loose-limb'd rest,
Lay peäle upon her mother's breast,
Her waxen eyelids seal'd her eyes
Vrom darksome trees, an' sheenèn skies,
An' halls a-hung wi' holm, that rung
Wi' many a tongue, o' wold an' young.

ROUND THINGS

A fairy ring as round's the sun
On our green meadow bends its rim,
Out where we saw the wavelings run
Across the pond with rounded brim.
And there by round-built ricks of hay,
By sun-heat burnt, by sunshine brown'd,
We met in merry ring to play,
All springing on, and wheeling round.

And there, as stones we chanc'd to fling
Swept out in flight a lofty bow,
And fell on water, ring by ring
Of waves bespread the pool below,
Beside the bridge's arch, that springs
Between the banks, within the brims,
Where swung the lowly-bending swings,
On elm-tree boughs, on mossy limbs.

DAWN

How fast it dawneth up the sky,
    Softly lighter, softly brighter
Tinging sides of clouds on high,
And the stream that rambles by.
What brings the day that I see break
To sleeping men or men that wake?

How fast it dawneth o'er the grass,
    Dimly shaded, dewy-bladed,
Where I see no lad or lass
O'er the dusky pathway pass.
But may ev'ry soul be gay
To sing and whistle through the day.

Show forth old home-ground with thy oak,
    Now so dim in stem and limb,
Come forth dear house with thy blue smoke,
And show thy doorway and thy folk;
Though the sun comes not to shine
On any early friends of mine.

Come orchard out from shade to light,
    Come apple trees, and hives of bees;
Rise Hambledon in thy blue height;
Come mead, and cows of red and white.
Though night dreams flee as here I roam,
Still let me dream myself at home.

THE MOOR

Where yonder leaning hill-side roves
    With woody dippings, far around,
And many jutting brows, and coves,
    Of rugged cliffs, and slopy ground,
Beside the stream that slowly sinks
    With reaches tinted from the skies,
    And stream-side meadows, lowly lies
The moor, with dikes and sedgy brinks.

About us there the willow shade
    Oft play'd beside the water's edge,
And there the rodded bulrush sway'd
    Its soft brown club, above the sedge,
And by the aspen or the bridge,
    The angler sat, and lightly whipp'd
    His little float, that, dancing, dipp'd
From o'er the waveling's little ridge.

There cows, in clusters, rambled wide,
    Some hanging low their heads to eat,
Some lying on their heavy side,
    Some standing on their two-peaked feet,
Some sheeted white, some dun or black,
    Some red, and others brindled dark,
    Some marked with milk-white star, or spark,
And ours all white along the back.

There cows, to others, low'd; now here,
    Now there, from open heat to shade;
And out among them, far or near,
    With quiv'ring scream, the horses neigh'd,
The while some boy, within the mead,
    On some high mare might come astride;
    And sliding down her bulging side,
Might set her, snorting, free to feed.

And there we saw the busy crow
    For mussels down the river play,
And rooks sweep on where men below
    Went, water hemm'd, their crooked way,
And gamb'ling boys, in merry train,
    On holidays came rambling by
    With often-grounded poles, to fly;
In high-bow'd flight, o'er dike and drain.

There men at work on pathless grass,
    Are seen, though out of hearing, wide,
By neighbour-meeting folk, that pass
    The many-roaded upland side.
So some may like the trampled road,
    O'er well-rubbed stile-bars, with a gloss,
    And some the moor, that some may cross
But pass no door of man's abode.

TREES

How fair's the summer sun that gleams
    O'er field and brook, and road and man;
How sweet's the summer wind that streams
    Where day gives glowing brows to fan,
And o'er the rose in open bloom,
    And o'er the nodding lily's whiteness,
Through the dingle's shadow gloom,
    And o'er the open downside's brightness.

As trees in three ways charm the mind,
    By hues that bloom or bough may show,
By shape, as comely of its kind,
    By lifelike swayings to and fro,
My love is mark'd by threefold praise
    For shapeliness all of comely meetness —
Comeliness of gait and ways,
    And all her mind's well-worded sweetness.

7. 'The skill that conceals skill'

Geoffrey Grigson believed that Barnes readers need 'to be peculiarly equipped, in a way not very common at present, in verse physiology, speech of "breath-sounded words", and in the felicities of rhythm' (Grigson 1962: 202). It is certainly the case that Barnes's poems, both in the Blackmoor dialect and in Standard English, are complex in their metre and also in their sound patterns. It is a subtle complexity. Barnes admired, he said, the 'skill that conceals skill' in Bardic poetry, and in his own work he achieved a similarly unobtrusive patterning, effectively supporting and developing his meanings within lines that 'keep all the strait rules of verse, yet flow as freely as if they were wholly untied' (Barnes 1867: 307).

Frequently, Barnes's sound patterns appear to have been used principally for their harmony and pleasant echo. His article, 'Thoughts on Beauty and Art' (1861), emphasises his pleasure in harmonious shapes of all kinds. *Awdlau*, for instance, or single rhyme, simply repeats the same word. In 'Winter a-comen' three lines of each stanza end on the same words and rhyme the previous word. (The fourth line rhymes throughout the poem).

> The zwallows have all a-hied away,
> The flowers have now a-died away,
> An' boughs, wi' their leaves a-dried away,
>   In wind do goo to an' fro.
>
> Your walks in the ash-tree droves be cwold,
> Your banks in the elem groves be cwold,
> Your bench by the house's oves be cwold
>   Where zummer did leätely glow.
> (PWB I: 573, stanzas 2 and 3)

Barnes also used Persian *ghazal rhyme* to link couplets: the same phrase is repeated, as in 'At Eve' (PWB II: 731), at the end of every second line.

Some of Barnes's sound patterns, however, may be used to more meaningful effect. In a lengthy discussion on rhyme, in *Philological Grammar,* Barnes appreciates the power of patterned sound to link and emphasise rhythms or ideas (Barnes 1854: 277-308). He achieved this himself in, for example, 'Our Fathers' Works', whose unusual patterns of sound appear to emphasise the secure connection of tradition by their repetition and by the symbolism of their tightly woven links.

> Zoo now mid nwone ov us *vorget*
> The pattern our vorefathers *ʒet*;
> But each be *faïn* to under*teäke*
> Zome work to *meäke* vor others' *gaïn*,
> That we mid *leäve* mwore good to *sheäre*,
> Less ills to *bear*, less souls to *grieve*,
> An' when our hands do vall to *rest*,
> It mid be vrom a work *a-blest*.
> (PWB I: 270; author's italics)

It seems appropriate, given his wish to preserve a secure and stable community, that Barnes should have placed his images of local life within the stability of such regular sounds and rhythms for, in the Bardic poetry he admired, these formed 'word locks' to help speaker and hearer note and remember its lines.

Barnes also explained in *Philological Grammar* that in his view Welsh *cynghanedd* — a form of alliteration which chimes consonants in a kind of echo within a line — has emotional resonances. Hertz (1985) finds semantic significance, both emotional and metaphorical, in its use in the last line of each stanza in Barnes's 'My Orcha'd in Linden Lea'. Hertz believes its rich euphony is suggestive here of the luxurious bounty that is the fruit weighing down an apple tree, a natural bounty that the speaker values much more than city riches.

> I be free to goo abrode,
> Or teäke ageän my hwomeward road
> To where, vor me, the apple tree
> Do leän down low in Linden Lea.
> (PWB I: 233)

Hertz also suggests that *cynghanedd* allowed Barnes to merge place names with people, as in 'Linda Deäne' (PWB I: 403) where the last line of each stanza refers to Linda Deäne of Ellendon and in 'Lindenore' (PWB I: 405) which features Ellen Dare of Lindenore. In Hertz's view the blending could be semiotically significant in that Barnes believed that places gained their importance from the people who lived in them.

Hertz finds a hint of semiotic significance too in 'Went Home', in a combination of internal rhyme and the concentration upon a key-word that is called Welsh *cymmeriad*. A traveller is going home and each stanza ends on the place name 'Meldonley', his journey's end. The final couplet of each verse contains a triple rhyme which Hertz calls a 'staircase' down which the poem's speaker can travel to his destination.

> Till I come down, vrom Meldon's crown
> To rufs o' brown, at Meldonley.
> (PWB I: 392)

On occasion, Barnes uses another technique, *parallelism*, to meaningful effect. Sometimes, as in 'The Fall', it achieves a rhythm and rhyme that is simply attractive and satisfying in its neat equivalence.

> The length o' the days ageän do shrink,
>   An' flowers be thin in meäd, among
>   The eegrass, a-sheenen bright, along
> *Brook upon brook, an' brink by brink.*
> (PWB II: 570; author's italics)

However, in 'The Wife a-lost', parallelism is used in more complex fashion in the final couplets of the first two stanzas, heightening, through the contrasts it identifies, the poignancy of courage displayed by a widower — surely Barnes himself, who lost his wife, Julia, in 1852. The speaker visits places he has not shared with his beloved because here, for a while, he can live his life without the suffering he feels amongst the trees and walks they enjoyed together:

> An' I don't look to meet ye now,
>   As I do look at hwome.

> An' I don't grieve to miss ye now,
>   As I do grieve at home.
> (PWB I: 333)

Still, Barnes did not follow patterns such as these slavishly or simplistically. Hardy wrote that 'by a felicitous instinct' his friend sometimes displayed in his poetry 'sudden irregularities as if feeling rebelled against further drill' (Hardy 1908: p.x). And in 'The Wife a-lost' the final couplets of the third and fourth stanzas take a different form, abandoning parallelism whilst still answering the imperative of the poem's overall *ababcdcd* rhyme scheme.

102

> An' I don't grieve to miss ye now,
> As I at hwome do pine.
>
> An' be a waïtèn vor me now,
> To come vor evermwore.
> (PWB I: 333)

Moreover, although the seventh line of each stanza ends on the word 'now', the significance of its meaning in the final stanza is subtly but crucially different from that in the preceding three. In the first three, 'now' relates to the speaker's experience of time suffered here on earth. In the fourth, it refers to time as it relates to the wife who has gone before and who is waiting — now — until her husband can join her for evermore.

Barnes also used rhyme, in a skilful and unobtrusive manner, in combination with metre, particularly in the monologues and dialogues of both his Non-standard and Standard poems. Sisson remarked: 'Such is Barnes's skill that the reality of the voice is enhanced, not lost, amidst intricacies of rhyme and metre' (Sisson 1965: 44-45). The poems certainly convey an impression of naturally occurring speech — 'and where else', Sisson continued, 'would you look for that in verse written in England in 1844?'. For one thing, the language becomes colloquial, in the Standard as well as in the Non-Standard poems. The Standard English poem, 'The Hines of Burnley' (PWB II: 697), begins with the remark, 'Well. Pleas'd or not it is all the same', which is hardly the stuff of conventional poetry. Furthermore, as in the following examples, even the single voice of the monologues gives the hearer a sense of dialogue through inclusive pronouns, and through direct address to a named person or to 'you'.

> Since we were striplèns naïghbour John,
> The good wold merry times be gone:
> ('Harvest Hwome'; PWB I: 137)
>
> Ah! yesterday, d'ye know, I voun'
> Tom Dumpy's cwoat an' smock-frock, down
> Below the pollard out in groun'.
> ('Polly be-èn Upzides wi' Tom'; PWB I: 127)

This last example even bears the hallmarks of ordinary talk in its exclamation and its filler, 'd'ye know'. Other poems include the familiar phrases of phatic communion, the semantically insignificant but socially important language used particularly to open and close conversations. Phatic openers can include ritual greetings, references to on-going work, and comments on the listener's appearance (Laver 1974). All these are present in Thomas's opening remarks to John in 'The Common a-took in'.

> Good morn t'ye, John. How b'ye? how b'ye?
> Zoo you be gwaïn to market, I do zee.
> Why, you be quite a-lwoaded wi' your geese.
> (PWB I: 158)

The naturally uneven pattern of this conversational starter somehow blends perfectly with the iambic feet of Barnes's chosen metre. The second and third lines quoted here each have one caesura, the first line has two. These breaks occur in varying positions. Such variation, together with run-on lines, also distracts from this poem's rhyme scheme — which is *aabb*, *abab*, or occasionally *abba* — so that its regularity, cutting across conversational turn-taking, is unobtrusive and the poetic does not overwhelm the apparently natural.

> JOHN Why, I'm a-gettèn rid ov ev'ry goose
> An' goslèn I've a-got: an' what is woose,
> I fear that I must zell my little cow.
>
> THOMAS How zoo, then, John? Why, what's the matter now?

But irregularity suggests not only spontaneous naturalness. Flexibility also allows Barnes to use rhythm, and in addition intonation, to convey emotion. Take, for example, the third stanza of 'Polly be-èn Upzides wi' Tom'. Polly tells her listeners that yesterday she took Tom's smock-frock whilst he was working and sewed the sleeves so that when he put it on his arms were pinioned behind him. He was not amused. She and her friends watched and laughed whilst

> ...he drow'd
> Hizzelf about, an' teäv'd, an' blow'd,
> Lik' any up-tied calf.
>
> Then in a veag away he flung
> His frock, an' after me he sprung,
> An' mutter'd out sich dreats, an' wrung
> His vist up sich a size!
> (PWB I: 127)

Here, rhythm and intonation help to convey Tom's fury as Polly observed it. The metrical feet are iambs. Yet the main emphases in the last four lines quoted here seem to be *veag, frock, sprung, dreats, vist, sich, size*. For the tone nuclei of these lines — the points at which intonation moves upwards or downwards in a stretch of speech between a suggestion of pause — do not coincide with each and every metrical stress. Instead, intonation moves on words which are introduced by /v/ /f/ /d/ /s/ and end in relatively hard sounding consonants, /g/ /k/, or the noisy /z/. A sense of tension — mounting tension — may be reinforced because the clause 'an' after me he sprung' has much the same intonational curve, in the same length of tone unit, as the following clause 'an' mutter'd out sich dreats'. Consequently, both can be uttered rapidly, the second emphasising the first in its repeated pattern. The next two tone units, which appear to be 'an' wrung / His vist up' and 'sich a size', more or less match each other in intonational curve but are metrically shorter and so may sound more agitated than the previous pair.

The impression of naturalness in poems such as this makes plain that although, as he explained in his *Philological Grammar* (1854), Barnes thought poets benefited by concentrating their energies within self-imposed metrical and rhyming tasks, he was always subtly creative within the discipline of these limits. As Hardy wrote in the Preface to his edition:

> Primarily spontaneous, he was academic closely after;...a far remove from the popular impression of him as the naïf and rude bard who sings only because he must, and who submits the uncouth lines of his page to us without knowing how they come there. (Hardy 1908: viii)

This skilful combination of the spontaneous with the deliberate is also discussed here in 'A "mellow" tone', the section which considers Barnes's ability, both in Non-standard and in Standard English, to suggest the mellow sounds that he found, and believed to indicate a mellow character, in the language of the Blackmoor community.

WOAK HILL

When sycamore leaves wer a-spreadèn,
　　Green-ruddy, in hedges,
Bezide the red doust o' the ridges,
　　A-dried at Woak Hill;

I packed up my goods all a-sheenèn
　　Wi' long years o' handlèn,
On dousty red wheels ov a waggon,
　　To ride at Woak Hill.

The brown thatchen ruf o' the dwellèn
　　I then wer a-leävèn,
Had shelter'd the sleek head o' Meäry,
　　My bride at Woak Hill.

But now vor zome years, her light voot-vall
　　'S a-lost vrom the vloorèn.
Too soon vor my jaÿ an' my childern,
　　She died at Woak Hill.

But still I do think that, in soul,
　　She do hover about us;
To ho vor her motherless childern,
　　Her pride at Woak Hill.

Zoo — lest she should tell me hereafter
　　I stole off 'ithout her,
An' left her, uncall'd at house-riddèn,
　　To bide at Woak Hill —

I call'd her so fondly, wi' lippèns
　　All soundless to others,
An' took her wi' aïr-reachèn hand,
　　To my zide at Woak Hill.

On the road I did look round, a-talkèn
　　To light at my shoulder,
An' then led her in at the door-way,
　　Miles wide vrom Woak Hill.

An' that's why vo'k thought, vor a season,
    My mind wer a-wandrèn
Wi' sorrow, when I wer so sorely
    A-tried at Woak Hill.

But no; that my Meäry mid never
    Behold herzelf slighted,
I wanted to think that I guided
    My guide vrom Woak Hill.

WENT HWOME

Upon the slope, the hedge did bound
The vield wi' blossom-whited zide,
An' charlock patches, yollow-dyed,
Did reach along the white-soil'd ground;
An' vo'k, a-comèn up vrom meäd,
    Brought gil'cup meal upon the shoe;
Or went on where the road did leäd,
    Wi' smeechy doust from heel to tooe,
As noon did smite, wi' burnèn light,
The road so white, to Meldonley.

An' I did tramp the zun-dried ground,
By hedge-climb'd hills, a-spread wi' flow'rs,
An' watershootèn dells, an' tow'rs,
By elem-trees a-hemm'd all round,
To zee a vew wold friends, about
    Wold Meldon, where I still ha' zome,
That bid me speed as I come out,
    An' now ha' bid me welcome hwome,
As I did goo, while skies wer blue,
Vrom view to view, to Meldonley.

An' there wer timber'd knaps, that show'd
Cool sheädes, vor rest, on grassy ground,
An' thatch-brow'd windows, flower-bound,
Where I could wish wer my abode.

I pass'd the maïd avore the spring,
    An' shepherd by the thornen tree;
An' heärd the merry drever zing,
    But met noo kith or kin to me,
'Till I come down, vrom Meldon's crown
To rufs o' brown, at Meldonley.

KEEPÈN UP O' CHRIS'MAS

An' zoo you didden come athirt,
To have zome fun last night: how wer't?
Vor we'd a-work'd wi' all our might
To scour the iron things up bright,
An' brush'd an' scrubb'd the house all drough;
An' brought in vor a brand, a plock
O' wood so big's an uppèn-stock,
An' hung a bough o' misseltoo,
An' ax'd a merry friend or two,
    To keepèn up o' Chris'mas.

An' there wer wold an' young; an' Bill,
Soon after dark, stalk'd up vrom mill.
An' when he wer a-comèn near,
He whissled loud vor me to hear;
Then roun' my head my frock I roll'd,
An' stood in orcha'd like a post,
To meäke en think I wer a ghost.
But he wer up to't, an' did scwold
To vind me stannèn in the cwold,
    A keepèn up o' Chris'mas.

We plaÿ'd at forfeits, an' we spun
The trencher roun', an' meäde such fun!
An' had a geäme o' dree-ceärd loo,
An' then begun to hunt the shoe.
An' all the wold vo'k zittèn near,
A-chattèn roun' the vier pleäce,
Did smile in woone another's feäce,
An' sheäke right hands wi' hearty cheer,
An' let their left hands spill their beer,
    A keepèn up o' Chris'mas.

ECLOGUE: THE COMMON A-TOOK IN

Thomas an' John

THOMAS

Good morn t'ye, John. How b'ye ? how b'ye ?
Zoo you be gwaïn to market, I do zee.
Why, you be quite a-lwoaded wi' your geese.

JOHN

Ees, Thomas, ees.
Why, I'm a-gettèn rid ov ev'ry goose
An' goslèn I've a-got: an' what is woose,
I fear that I must zell my little cow.

THOMAS

How zoo, then, John ? Why, what's the matter now ?
What, can't ye get along ? B'ye run a-ground ?
An' can't paÿ twenty shillèns vor a pound ?
What, can't ye put a lwoaf on shelf?

JOHN

                    Ees, now;
But I do fear I shan't 'ithout my cow.
No; they do meän to teäke the moor in, I do hear,
An' 'twill be soon begun upon;
Zoo I must zell my bit o' stock to-year,
Because they woon't have any groun' to run upon.

THOMAS

Why, what d'ye tell o'? I be very zorry
To hear what they be gwaïn about;
But yet I s'pose there'll be a 'lotment vor ye,
When they do come to mark it out.

JOHN

No; not vor me, I fear. An' if there should,
Why 'twoulden be so handy as 'tis now;
Vor 'tis the common that do do me good,
The run for my vew geese, or vor my cow.

THOMAS
Ees, that's the job; why 'tis a handy thing
To have a bit o' common, I do know,
To put a little cow upon in Spring,
The while woone's bit ov orcha'd grass do grow.

JOHN
Aye, that's the thing, you zee. Now I do mow
My bit o' grass, an' meäke a little rick;
An' in the zummer, while do grow,
My cow do run in common vor to pick
A bleäde or two o' grass, if she can vind em,
Vor tother cattle don't leäve much behind em.
Zoo in the evenèn, we do put a lock
O' nice fresh grass avore the wicket;
An' she do come at vive or zix o'clock,
As constant as the zun, to pick it.
An' then, bezides the cow, why we do let
Our geese run out among the emmet hills;
An' then when we do pluck em, we do get
Vor zeäle zome veathers an' zome quills;
An' in the winter we do fat em well,
An' car em to the market vor to zell
To gentlevo'ks, vor we don't oft avvword
To put a goose a-top ov ouer bwoard;
But we do get our feäst,—vor we be eäble
To clap the giblets up a-top o' teäble.

THOMAS
An' I don't know o' many better things,
Than geese's heads and gizzards, lags an' wings.

JOHN
An' then, when I ha' nothèn else to do,
Why I can teäke my hook an' gloves, an' goo
To cut a lot o' vuzz and briars
Vor hetèn ovens, or vor lightèn viers.
An' when the childern be too young to eärn
A penny, they can g'out in zunny weather,
An' run about, an' get together
A bag o' cow-dung vor to burn.

THOMAS
'Tis handy to live near a common;
But I've a-zeed, an' I've a-zaid,
That if a poor man got a bit o' bread,
They'll try to teäke it vrom en.
But I wer twold back tother day,
That they be got into a way
O' lettèn bits o' groun' out to the poor.

JOHN
Well, I do hope 'tis true, I'm sure;
An' I do hope that they will do it here,
Or I must goo to workhouse, I do fear.

POLLY BE-ÈN UPZIDES WI' TOM

Ah! yesterday, d'ye know, I voun'
Tom Dumpy's cwoat an' smock-frock, down
Below the pollard out in groun';
    An' zoo I slyly stole
An' took the smock-frock up, an' tack'd
The sleeves an' collar up, an' pack'd
Zome nice sharp stwones, all fresh a-crack'd
    'Ithin each pocket-hole.

An' in the evenèn, when he shut
Off work, an' come an' donn'd his cwoat,
Their edges gi'ed en sich a cut,
    How we did stan' an' laugh!
An' when the smock-frock I'd a-zow'd
Kept back his head an' hands, he drow'd
Hizzelf about, an' teäv'd, an' blow'd,
    Lik' any up-tied calf.

Then in a veag away he flung
His frock, an' after me he sprung,
An' mutter'd out sich dreats, an' wrung
    His vist up sich a size!

But I, a-runnèn, turn'd an' drow'd
Some doust, a-pick'd up vrom the road,
Back at en wi' the wind, that blow'd
    It right into his eyes.

An' he did blink, an' vow he'd catch
Me zomehow yet, an' be my match.
But I wer nearly down to hatch
    Avore he got vur on;
An' up in chammer, nearly dead
Wi' runnèn, lik' a cat I vled,
An' out o' window put my head
    To zee if he were gone.

An' there he wer, a-prowlèn roun'
Upon the green; an' I look'd down
An' told en that I hoped he voun'
    He mussen think to peck
Upon a body zoo, nor whip
The meäre to drow me off, nor tip
Me out o' cart ageän, nor slip
    Cut hoss-heäir down my neck.

RIVERS DON'T GI'E OUT

The brook I left below the rank
Ov alders that do sheäde his bank,
A-runnèn down to dreve the mill
Below the knap, 's a-runnèn still;
The creepèn days an' weeks do vill
    Up years, an' meäke wold things o' new,
    An' vok' do come, an' live, an' goo,
    But rivers don't gi'e out, John.

The leaves that in the spring do shoot
So green, in fall be under voot;
Maÿ flow'rs do grow vor June to burn,
An' milk-white blooth o' trees do kern,
An' ripen on, an' vall in turn;

The miller's moss-green wheel mid rot,
An' he mid die an' be vorgot,
But rivers don't gi'e out, John.

A vew short years do bring an' rear
A maïd—as Jeäne wer—young an' feäir,
An' vewer zummer-ribbons, tied
In Zunday knots, do feäde bezide
Her cheäk avore her bloom ha' died:
  Her youth won't staÿ,—her rwosy look
  'S a feädèn flow'r, but time's a brook
  To run an' not gi'e out, John.

An' yet, while things do come an' goo,
God's love is steadvast, John, an' true;
If winter vrost do chill the ground,
'Tis but to bring the zummer round,
All's well a-lost where He's a-vound,
  Vor if 'tis right, vor Christes seäke
  He'll gi'e us mwore than He do teäke,—
  His goodness don't gi'e out, John.

WALK AND TALK

Come up the grove, where softly blow
The winds, o'er dust, and not with snow,
A-sighing through the leafless thorn,
But not o'er flow'rs or eary corn,
Though still the walk is in the lew
Beside the gapless hedge of yew,
And wind-proof ivy, hanging thick
On oaks beside the tawny rick;
And let us talk an hour away
While softly sinks the dying day.

Now few at evening are the sounds
Of life, on roads or moon-paled grounds;
So low be here our friendly words
While still'd around are men and birds,

Nor startle we the night that dims
The world to men of weary limbs;
But let us tell in voices low
Our little tales, lest wind may blow
Their flying sounds too far away,
To ears yet out as ends the day.

For what we tell, and what we own,
Are ours, and dear to us alone,
Past joys, so sweet in after thought,
And hopes that yet may come to naught;
But wherefore should we not look on
To happy days till all are gone?
For if the day, so fair in dreams,
Should come less fair than now it seems,
Yet while a foreseen day seems gay
We have at once that happy day.

BEECHLEY

Oh! the beech lawns at Beechley, how charming they wound
By the long eastern landridge of highwooded ground;
And its low-lying dingle, with wandering rill,
And low-leaning beech-lawns, that reached to the hill;
    May its dairies do well,
      And may God speed its plough,
    For those I knew dwell there,
      But where are they now?

And there stood the houses, some high and some small,
With their flow'r-warding pales and their rose-behung wall,
And westward and northward outsprang a long streech
Of grass-land, bestudded with elm and with beech.
    And late in the day,
      Some maid by her cow
    Was singing full gay there,
      But where is she now?

And there, in the dusk, in fine weather, we played
At our game 'Hide and seek' in the nook and the shade,
With 'I spy,' or 'Run yonder,' or 'Am I not near,
Jane Hunt or John Hine?' or 'Ha! ha! you are here;'
    Or cunning Ned Knoles,
      By stall or by mow,
    Finds out such queer holes there,
      And where is he now?

Or at cricket, while one, in a quick-handed fight
With the ball, saw in glory his wicket upright,
The ball fleetly roll'd and it sprang, and it flew,
It was out in the field, and at home at the shoe;
    Or it hit a man out,
      Oh! he could not tell how;
    While others would shout there
      'Well where are you now?'

'Tis long since my footsteps have trodden the ground
Where few, I should fear, of my friends would be found.
But tell me, I pray you, all ever you can
Of the life and the loss of the maid and the man,
    The Hinds, and the Harleys,
      Oh! How are they? How?
    And the Burnleys and Deans; there
      Oh! where are they now?

HOME FROM A JOURNEY

Back home on my mare I took my way,
Through hour upon hour of waning day,
Where thistles on windy ledges shook,
And aspen leaves quiver'd o'er the brook,
By slope and by level ambling on,
Till day with the sunken sun was gone,
And out in the west a sheet of light
Was lingering pale—pale in the night.

At last, as my mare came snorting near
My dwelling, where all things near were dear,
The apples were swung in darksome balls,
And roses hung dark beside the walls,
No cows were about the fields to low,
The fowls were at roost in sleeping row,
And only the rushing owl came by
In moongleamings pale—pale in the sky.

Within my old door my lamp was clear,
To show me the faces many and dear,
My mother's, now dimm'd by life-long care,
My wife's, as a wife's, of ten years' wear,
My children's, well shapen line by line,
One seven, one five, one three years, mine,
And one that has come before our sight,
His one moon pale—pale in the night.

8. The Hardy connection

Thomas Hardy, whose family lived in the Dorset village of Upper Bockhampton, was not sent to William Barnes's Dorchester school because the fees were too expensive for his stone-mason father (Hearl 1966: 274). But Hardy came to know Barnes in the late 1850s whilst studying under the architect John Hicks, whose office was next door to the school. Hardy would often call on Barnes to ask for the older man's advice and remained acquainted with him throughout his life. Perhaps the relationship influenced the shaping of some of Hardy's fictional scenes and characters. Is there something of the young William, looking beyond the land of his farming family to a life of learning, in Jude Fawley dreaming of Christminster? Was the 'popular school at Casterbridge', referred to in one of Hardy's *Wessex Tales,* 'Interlopers at the Knap', Barnes's establishment? Could Hardy have had local enthusiasm for Barnes' dialect writing in mind when, in *The Mayor of Casterbridge,* local labourers admired Farfrae's enthusiastic singing of home in his own Scottish dialect? For to them Farfrae seemed 'like the poet of a new school who...is the first to articulate what all his listeners have felt, though but dimly till then' (Hardy 1978: 121-122), and Hardy had written in *The Athenaeum* of the delight with which Barnes's readings of his own dialect works were received in the local Town Halls, a delight which could 'hardly be imagined by readers of his lines acquainted only with English in its customary form' (1886: 502).

Dialect certainly preoccupied Hardy. His local characters speak an approximation of a local speech (not a precise rendering like Barnes's). But Bernard Jones points out that their dialect is not a rough imitation of Barnes's: 'Hardy was a Dorchester man...[and the] dialect Barnes had in mind when writing the dialect poems was that spoken around Sturminster Newton in the early years of the century' (PWB I: 17). Moreover, Hardy's attitude to dialect was more complex than Barnes's unqualified approval. Hardy insisted that his family knew but did not speak the local dialect except to the cottagers and workmen (Page 1980: 153). So perhaps his authorial perspective is not entirely ironic when Henchard, Hardy's fictional Mayor of Casterbridge, speaks disparagingly of his daughters' local words, calling them 'those terrible marks of the beast' (Hardy 1978: 200). But it is more probable that any objection Hardy had was not to dialect itself but to what he called a 'sad hash' of language, the kind of mix of Standard and local dialect that resulted from National School teachers bringing their own English to rural areas and producing, he argued in *The Dorsetshire Labourer* (1883), a composite language without harmony. Certainly, Tess's tragic journey, in *Tess of the d'Urbervilles,* from her harsh but relatively innocent labouring origins to her seduction, rejection and death in a hostile middle-class world, was paralleled by her move from local speech to a language influenced by the Standard words and meanings of her betrayers (Shepherd 1990: 52-53).

But Barnes's language was no sad hash. Hardy wrote approvingly of his friend's work, acknowledging his faithful adherence to a 'fast-perishing language' (Hardy 1908: viii). He also rememembered Barnes with affection in his poem 'The Last Signal: A Memory of William Barnes' (Gibson 1976: 473). Walking through the fields from his home at Max Gate towards Came Rectory, from which Barnes's funeral procession was leaving, Hardy caught sight of a flash of reflected sunlight 'mirrored by the coffin of my friend there'. He saw the 'brief blaze' as a sign of farewell from Barnes, like 'a wave of his hand'. But the farewell glow of light, described in the poem, could also be a metaphor of the sunlit landscape of Barnes's writing, the brilliant colour of its fields and flowers, the cheerful equanimity of the people working the land. For Barnes's poems, concerning themes which Hardy believed would 'in some not remote time...be familiar to nobody' (Hardy 1908: viii), are a last signal to readers of a way of living that was passing during Barnes's own lifetime. His regret at its passing, at the loss of rural peace and culture as increasing poverty and movement to the cities disrupted tradition and harmony, shadows — yet does not overwhelm — the sunlight of his work. So it is appropriate that Barnes's signal of light should flash from 'amid the shadow of that livid sad east', brightening the dark cloud that Hardy observed as the 'sun sloped low down to westward'.

The poem is also a 'last signal' of Barnes in that its language and construction is reminiscent of his own work. The coffin carries Barnes on his 'grave-way' and this compound is typical of Barnes's own word-building, his preference (discussed here in 'Circles of language') for neologisms made from the morphemes he considered to be pure English rather than borrowings from other languages. Hardy's rhyme scheme — matching the last syllable of each stanza's first line with one in the middle of the next as well as rhyming every second with every fourth — is also representative of Barnes's constant use of complex patterning.

Of course such features are also typical of Hardy's own work, but perhaps to some extent they are present in his poems as a result of Barnes's influence. For Hardy was the younger man, beginning to write long after Barnes's own poems were first published, and Florence Hardy describes a relationship in which Barnes had a great deal to offer, teaching Hardy 'the craftsman's ideal, to create for the pleasure derived from a skilful alliance between imagination, brain and hand' (F.E. Hardy 1962: 322). It might be argued that Hardy achieved far greater skill than Barnes in his poetry because the patterning of his form is more sophisticated in its balance between the expected and the unexpected. Yet Hardy himself, as he acknowledged in the preface to his 1908 collection of his friend's work, recognised and admired in Barnes the capacity (discussed here in 'The skill that conceals skill') to break into patterns with effective irregularities, 'as if feeling rebelled against further drill' (Hardy 1908: px).

The question of control versus feeling is raised again, but in a contrastingly critical way, if another Hardy poem, 'The Collector Cleans his Picture' (Gibson 1976: 617), has anything to do with Barnes. The poem does not directly implicate Barnes, but its persona resembles him insofar as this man is also a rural parson and his hobby is collecting and cleaning pictures, a pastime which Barnes himself enjoyed. Barnes's daughter, Lucy, wrote that her father delighted in searching in antique shops for a painting covered with blackened varnish and would then

> retire to his den, and subject [it] to a mysterious process...which filled the house with the smell of oils and varnish. After some days he would come downstairs with a beaming face and display the astonishing results of his labour (Scott 1887: 151-152).

But is there any link between Hardy's collector and Barnes, other than a coincidence of hobbies? In the preface to his Barnes collection, Hardy remarks that his friend managed to 'elude in his verse those dreams and speculations that cannot leave alone the mystery of things' (Hardy 1908: xi). Yet if the art collector of Hardy's imagination is based in any significant way on Barnes, then such dreams and speculations were not entirely unknown to him. For Hardy's parson has found in 'the rooms of a trader in ancient house-gear' the kind of painting, 'murked with grimefilms', that Barnes himself liked to clean, and late one Saturday night he sets to work. To his delight he eventually uncovers from beneath the dirt the first hints of an erotic female form, maybe 'the ranker Venus'. Kneeling before the picture, the parson 'kissed the panel, / Drunk with the lure of love's inhibited dreamings'. He works on until dawn but then, to his horror, the final revelation that slowly emerges is of 'A hag... / Pointing the slanted finger towards a bosom / Eaten away of a rot from the lusts of a lifetime...'. Aghast, the parson sits stunned and despairing — till he is 'roused by a clear-voiced bell-chime' calling him to matins.

So, if the match between the poem's parson and Barnes does go beyond a mere liking for picture restoring, did Hardy see in his friend's infinite capacity to find beauty in rural life something more complex, inhibited and knowingly evasive? Probably any connection between the 'The Collector Cleans his Picture' and William Barnes is not so direct. It is true that Barnes's poems do not probe below the surface of a relatively simple view of life. But there is no hint from his biographers of anything other than a genuinely straightforward, courageous and generous-spirited man. Moreover, the judgemental edge in Hardy's poem is not present in his own overt references to Barnes's avoidance of speculation. For he says, of the mystery that Barnes avoids, that it is 'possibly an unworthy mystery and disappointing if solved'. Yet he admits that it has 'a harrowing fascination for many poets'. So is the link between the poem and Barnes, if any exists, a blending of Hardy's own complexities with the simpler self of a man he remembered with both admiration — and, maybe, a touch of envy?

Perhaps this hint of a connection between the two men is also a mystery not worthy of investigation. What is certain, however, is that some of Hardy's poems appear to have been written with specific examples of Barnes' work in mind. For instance, Zietlow points out (1969) that Hardy's 'To a Motherless Child' (Gibson 1976: 65) is very similar in content to Barnes's earlier poem, 'The Motherless Child' (PWB I: 251). But, Zietlow argues, Hardy's version of this poem, and others, is critically different in attitude to adversity. It is true that the speaker in Barnes's 'The Motherless Child' finds comfort in his daughter's face because, so like her dead mother's, it seems to bring his wife back to him, whilst in Hardy's poem the daughter's likeness to her mother does not ease the widower's loss. However, neither Barnes's life, nor his poems overall, suggest a shallow turning from grief. Rather his work implies a man who felt pain deeply but was determined to live his life with courage, like the widower in 'The Wife a-lost' (PWB I: 333) who, though he carries on his day to day existence by avoiding the places he had known and loved with his wife, does so in full awareness of the suffering he feels at her loss.

Nonetheless, an erroneous impression that Barnes lacked depth and critical judgement could be fostered by Hardy's own edition of his friend's work, for he adjusted a number of the poems he selected in ways which reduce the scope of their vision. These alterations are of three kinds. (The full texts of examples of these poems are given in this Trent edition.)

First, some reduce the personal detail of a poem. For instance, in Hardy's edition, 'Haÿ-carrèn' (PWB I: 115) and 'Spring' (PWB I: 295) have lost stanzas which, in the midst of landscape description, refer to a figure called Jenny. Hardy's version of 'Chris'mas Invitation' (PWB I: 176) is without its second stanza, the only one in the poem which refers to a particular individual, a sister, and a mundane detail about keeping her frock clean.

The second kind of cut removes stanzas referring to change. In Hardy's edition, 'The Settle an' the Girt Wood Vire' (PWB I: 173) is without a stanza which turns from contemplation of the settle and fire, as they used to be before the advent of small modern-day fireplaces, and talks of the domestic problems caused by dirty feet on new-fangled carpets. 'The Girt Wold House o' Mossy Stwone' (PWB I: 222) loses ll 19-26 which talk about inferior new housing and ll 5-14 which briefly describe the history of the old house's ownership, passing from the squire, when he died without heirs, to the speaker's grandfather and then to his father.

Thirdly, other omissions modify a religious tone. Hardy disliked what he called Barnes's tendency to write 'parsonically' (Hardy and Pinion 1972: 98), a tendency that manifested itself in the final stanzas of several poems by linking all that has gone before with an affirmation of God's goodness. So 'The Spring' (PWB I: 71), for example, loses its last two verses in Hardy's edition. These stanzas insist that the beauty and contentment of the natural world should remind onlookers, since their happiness was God's intention, that any misery they endure is of their own sinful making. The result of the cut is an essentially descriptive poem.

In fact, the majority of Hardy's cuts produce poems which are simply descriptive. These poems may have gained strength through their increased concentration on the landscape, but they lose elements — the references to individuals, to tradition and change, and to a moral perspective — which are representative of Barnes' character, thinking and art. For his is a peopled landscape, its interest for Barnes as much dependent upon those individuals who work with and contemplate nature as upon its intrinsic beauty. And to him the traditions, buildings and roads created by those who had gone before were blessings in the lives of their descendants and reminders that each new generation should pass to the next the fruits of its labours. As for the 'parsonical' stanzas, these are an essential part of Barnes's poetic purpose, his desire to set forth in verse 'the good and the loveworthy that men's minds would more readily take and hold it' (Levy 1960: 17).

The connection between Hardy and Barnes is therefore complex. It would seem that Hardy's work was influenced to an extent by Barnes. Barnes's reputation will have been shaped to a degree by Hardy's selective edition. However, though Hardy may not have been completely accurate in his representation of his friend's work, his assessment of the older man's achievement was wholly supportive. His poems, Hardy wrote, would continue to be read when much English literature had been forgotten (Hardy 1939).

HAŸ-CARRÈN

Tis merry ov a zummer's day,
When vo'k be out a-haulèn haÿ,
Where boughs, a-spread upon the ground,
Do meäke the staddle big an' round;
An' grass do stand in pook, or lie
In long-back'd weäles or parsels, dry.
There I do vind it stir my heart
To hear the frothèn hosses snort,
A-haulen on, wi' sleek heäir'd hides,
The red-wheel'd waggon's deep-blue zides.
Aye; let me have woone cup o' drink,
An' hear the linky harness clink,
An' then my blood do run so warm,
An' put sich strangth 'ithin my eärm,
That I do long to toss a pick,
A-pitchèn or a-meäkèn rick.

The bwoy is at the hosse's head,
An' up upon the waggon bed
The lwoaders, strong o' eärm do stan',
At head, an' back at taïl, a man,
Wi' skill to build the lwoad upright
An' bind the vwolded corners tight;
An' at each zide o'm, sprack an' strong,
A pitcher wi' his long-stemm'd prong,
Avore the best two women now
A-call'd to reäky after plough.

When I do pitchy, 'tis my pride
Vor Jenny Hine to reäke my zide,
An' zee her fling her reäke, an' reach
So vur, an' teäke in sich a streech;
An' I don't shatter haÿ, an' meäke
Mwore work than needs vor Jenny's reäke.
I'd sooner zee the weäles' high rows
Lik' hedges up above my nose,
Than have light work myzelf, an' vind
Poor Jeäne a-beät an' left behind;
Vor she would sooner drop down dead,
Than let the pitchers get a-head.

'Tis merry at the rick to zee
How picks do wag, an' haÿ do vlee.
While woone's unlwoadèn, woone do teäke
The pitches in; an' zome do meäke
The lofty rick upright an' roun',
An' tread en hard, an' reäke en down,
An' tip en, when the zun do zet,
To shoot a sudden vall o' wet.
An' zoo 'tis merry any day
Where vo'k be out a-carrèn haÿ.

THE SETTLE AN' THE GIRT WOOD VIRE

Ah! naïghbour John, since I an' you
Wer youngsters, ev'ry thing is new.
My father's vires wer all o' logs
O' cleft-wood, down upon the dogs
Below our clavy, high, an' brode
Enough to teäke a cart an' lwoad,
Where big an' little all zot down
At bwoth zides, an' bevore, all roun'.
An' when I zot among em, I
Could zee all up ageän the sky
Drough chimney, where our vo'k did hitch
The zalt-box an' the beäcon-vlitch,
An' watch the smoke on out o' vier,
All up an' out o' tun, an' higher.
An' there wer beäcon up on rack,
An' pleätes an' dishes on the tack;
An' roun' the walls wer heärbs a-stowed
In peäpern bags, an' blathers blowed.
An' just above the clavy-bwoard
Wer father's spurs, an' gun, an' sword;
An' there wer then, our girtest pride,
The settle by the vier zide.
    Ah! gi'e me, if I wer a squier,
    The settle an' the girt wood vier.

But they've a-wall'd up now wi' bricks
The vier pleäce vor dogs an' sticks,
An' only left a little hole
To teäke a little greäte o' coal,
So small that only twos or drees
Can jist push in an' warm their knees.
An' then the carpets they do use,
Ben't fit to tread wi' ouer shoes;
An' chairs an' couches be so neat,
You mussen teäke em vor a seat:
They be so fine, that vo'k mus' pleäce
All over em an' outer ceäse,
An' then the cover, when 'tis on,
Is still too fine to loll upon.
     Ah! gi'e me, if I wer a squier,
     The settle an' the girt wood vier.

Carpets, indeed! You coulden hurt
The stwone-vloor wi' a little dirt;
Vor what wer brought in doors by men,
The women soon mopp'd out ageän.
Zoo we did come vrom muck an' mire,
An' walk in straïght avore the vier;
But now, a man's a-kept at door
At work a pirty while, avore
He's screäp'd an' rubb'd, an' cleän and fit
To goo in where his wife do zit.
An' then if he should have a whiff
In there, 'twould only breed a miff:
He can't smoke there, vor smoke woon't goo
'Ithin the footy little flue.
     Ah! gi'e me, if I wer a squier,
     The settle an' the girt wood vier.

THE SPRING

When wintry weather's all a-done,
An' brooks do sparkle in the zun,
An' naïsy-buildèn rooks do vlee
Wi' sticks toward their elem tree;
When birds do zing, an' we can zee
    Upon the boughs the buds o' spring,—
    Then I'm as happy as a king,
      A-vield wi' health an' zunsheen.

Vor then the cowslip's hangèn flow'r
A-wetted in the zunny show'r,
Do grow wi' vi'lets, sweet o' smell,
Bezide the wood-screen'd grægle's bell;
Where drushes' aggs, wi' sky-blue shell,
    Do lie in mossy nest among
    The thorns, while they do zing their zong
      At evenèn in the zunsheen.

An' God do meäke his win' to blow
An' raïn to vall vor high an' low,
An' bid his mornèn zun to rise
Vor all alike, an' groun' an' skies
Ha' colors vor the poor man's eyes:
    An' in our trials He is near,
    To hear our mwoan an' zee our tear,
      An' turn our clouds to zunsheen.

An' many times when I do vind
Things all goo wrong, an' vo'k unkind,
To zee the happy veedèn herds,
An' hear the zingèn o' the birds,
Do soothe my sorrow mwore than words;
    Vor I do zee that 'tis our sin
    Do meäke woone's soul so dark 'ithin,
      When God would gi'e woone zunsheen.

THE MOTHERLESS CHILD

The zun'd a-zet back tother night,
    But in the zettèn pleäce
The clouds, a-redden'd by his light,
    Still glow'd avore my feäce.
An' I've a-lost my Meäry's smile,
I thought; but still I have her chile,
Zoo like her, that my eyes can treäce
The mother's in her daughter's feäce.
    O little feäce so near to me,
An' like thy mother's gone; why need I zay
Sweet night cloud, wi' the glow o' my lost day,
    Thy looks be always dear to me.

The zun'd a-zet another night;
    But, by the moon on high,
He still did zend us back his light
    Below a cwolder sky.
My Meäry's in a better land
I thought, but still her chile's at hand,
An' in her chile she'll zend me on
Her love, though she herzelf's a-gone.
    O little chile so near to me,
An' like thy mother gone; why need I zay,
Sweet moon, the messenger vrom my lost day,
    Thy looks be always dear to me.

TO A MOTHERLESS CHILD

Ah, child, thou art but half thy darling mother's;
    Hers couldst thou wholly be,
My light in thee would outglow all in others;
    She would relive to me.
But niggard Nature's trick of birth
    Bars, lest she overjoy,
Renewal of the loved on earth
    Save with alloy.

The Dame has no regard, alas, my maiden,
    For love and loss like mine —
No sympathy with mindsight memory-laden;
    Only with fickle eyne.
To her mechanical artistry
    My dreams are all unknown,
And why I wish that thou couldst be
    But One's alone!

                        Thomas Hardy

THE COLLECTOR CLEANS HIS PICTURE

Fili hominis, ecce ego tollo a te desiderabile oculorum tuorum in
    plaga. — EZECH, XXIV 16

    How I remember cleaning that strange picture!...
I had been deep in duty for my sick neighbour —
He besides my own — over several Sundays,
Often, too, in the week; so with parish pressures,
Baptisms, burials, doctorings, conjugal counsel —
All the whatnots asked of a rural parson —
Faith, I was well-nigh broken, should have been fully
Saving for one small secret relaxation,
One that in mounting manhood had grown my hobby.

    This was to delve at whiles for easel-lumber,
Stowed in the backmost slums of a soon-reached city,
Merely on chance to uncloak some worthy canvas,
Panel, or plaque, blacked blind by uncouth adventure,
Yet under all concealing a precious artfeat.
Such I had found not yet. My latest capture
Came from the rooms of a trader in ancient house-gear
Who had no scent of beauty or soul for brushcraft.
Only a tittle it cost — murked with grimefilms,
Gatherings of slow years, thick-varnished over,
Never a feature manifest of man's painting.

So, one Sunday, time ticking hard on midnight
Ere an hour subserved, I set me upon it.
Long with coiled-up sleeves I cleaned and yet cleaned,
Till a first fresh spot, a high light, looked forth,
Then another, like fair flesh, and another;
Then a curve, a nostril, and next a finger,
Tapering, shapely, significantly pointing slantwise.
'Flemish?' I said. 'Nay, Spanish.... But, nay, Italian!'
— Then meseemed it the guise of the ranker Venus,
Named of some Astarte, of some Cotytto.
Down I knelt before it and kissed the panel,
Drunk with the lure of love's inhibited dreamings.

Till the dawn I rubbed, when there leered up at me
A hag, that had slowly emerged from under my hands there,
Pointing the slanted finger towards a bosom
Eaten away of a rot from the lusts of a lifetime...
— I could have ended myself at the lashing lesson!
Stunned I sat till roused by a clear-voiced bell-chime,
Fresh and sweet as the dew-fleece under my luthern.
It was the matin service calling to me
From the adjacent steeple.

Thomas Hardy

THE LAST SIGNAL

(11 Oct. 1886)
A Memory of William Barnes

Silently I footed by an uphill road
That led from my abode to a spot yew-boughed;
Yellowly the sun sloped low down to westward,
    And dark was the east with cloud.

Then, amid the shadow of that livid sad east,
    Where the light was least, and a gate stood wide,
Something flashed the fire of the sun that was facing it,
    Like a brief blaze on that side.

Looking hard and harder I knew what it meant —
The sudden shine sent from the livid east scene;
It meant the west mirrored by the coffin of my friend there,
    Turning to the road from his green,

To take his last journey forth — he who in his prime
Trudged so many a time from that gate athwart the land!
Thus a farewell to me he signalled on his grave-way,
    As with a wave of his hand.

Winterborne-Came Path
                        Thomas Hardy

References and further reading

Abbott, C.C. (1938), ed., *Further Letters of Gerard Manley Hopkins*, London, Oxford University Press.

Barnes, W. (1830), 'Corruptions of the English Language', *Gentleman's Magazine*, June, 501-503.

Barnes, W. (1831), 'On English Derivatives', *Gentleman's Magazine*, June, 500.

Barnes, W. (1832), 'Compounds in the English Language', *Gentleman's Magazine*, Supplementary Vol. 102, 269.

Barnes, W. (1841), 'English Philology', *Gentleman's Magazine*, May, 510-511.

Barnes, W. (1844), *Poems of Rural Life in the Dorset Dialect*, with Dissertation on the Dorset Dialect, London, John Russell Smith.

Barnes, W. (1847), *Poems of Rural Life in the Dorset Dialect*, second edition with enlarged Dissertation and Glossary, London, John Russell Smith.

Barnes, W. (1849), 'The Nature and Use of Money', *Gentleman's Magazine*, January, 54.

Barnes, W. (1854), *A Philological Grammar*, London, John Russell Smith.

Barnes, W. (1859), *Views of Labour and Gold*, London, John Russell Smith.

Barnes, W. (1859), *Hwomely Rhymes*, second Dialect collection, London, John Russell Smith. (An 1863 edition is published as *Poems of Rural Life in the Dorset Dialect*.)

Barnes, W. (1861), 'Thoughts on Beauty and Art', *MacMillan's Magazine*, 4, 126-137.

Barnes, W. (1862) *Poems of Rural Life in the Dorset Dialect*, third Dorset dialect collection, London, John Russell Smith.

Barnes, W. (1867), 'The Old Bardic Poetry', *MacMillan's Magazine*, August, 306-317.

Barnes, W. (1879), *Poems of Rural Life in the Dorset Dialect*, a compilation of the 1844, 1859 and 1862 volumes, London, Kegan Paul.

Barrell, J. and Bull, J. (1982), eds.,*The Penguin Book of English Pastoral Verse*, Harmondsworth, Penguin.

Carlyle, T. (1843), *Past and Present*, London, Chapman and Hall.

Cassirer, E. (1946), *Language and Myth*, trans. S. Langer, New York, Dover.

Forster, E.M. (1951), *Two Cheers for Democracy*, London, Edward Arnold and Co.

Forsyth, R.A. (1967), 'The Conserving Myth of William Barnes', in *Romantic Mythologies*, edited by Ian Fletcher, London, Routledge and Kegan Paul, 137-168.

Gibson, J. (1976), *The Complete Poems of Thomas Hardy*, London, Papermac.

Gombrich, E.H. (1978 edition), *The Story of Art*, Phaidon Press, Oxford.

Grigson, G. (1950), *Selected Poems of William Barnes*, London, Routledge and Kegan Paul.

Grigson, G. (1962), 'Out of the Swim', *New Statesman*, 64, August 17, 202.

Hardy, F.E. (1962), first published 1928 and 1930, *The Life of Thomas Hardy*, London, Macmillan.

Hardy, E. and Pinion, F.B. (1972), *One Rare Fair Woman*, London, Macmillan.

Hardy, T. (1879), 'Poems of Rural Life in the Dorset Dialect', *New Quarterly Magazine*, October, 469-473.

Hardy, T. (1886), 'The Rev. W. Barnes, B.D.', *Athenaeum*, October, 501-502.

Hardy, T. (1908), *Select Poems of William Barnes*, London, Froude.

Hardy, T. (1939), 'Homage to William Barnes', *New Statesman* , December 9.

Hardy, T. (1978), first published 1886, *The Mayor of Casterbridge*, Harmondsworth, Penguin.

Hertz, A. (1985), 'The Hallowed Pleäces of William Barnes', *Victorian Poetry*, 23, No. 2, 109-214.

Hinchy, F.S. and V.M. (1966), *The Dorset William Barnes*, Blandford, Dorset, F.S. and V.M. Hinchy.

Jones, B. (1962), ed., *The Poems of William Barnes*, vols. 1 and 2, Carbondale, Illinois, Southern Illinois University Press.

Kilvert, F. (1944), first published in 3 volumes, 1938, 1939, 1940, *Kilvert's Diary*, London, J. Cape.

Laver, J. (1974), 'Communicative functions in phatic communion', in *The Organiation of Behaviour in Face-to-Face Interaction*, edited by A. Kendon, R.N. Harris, and M.R. Key, Mouton, The Hague.

Lawson, J.N. (1971), facsimile reproduction with an introduction by J. N. Lawson, *Robert Bloomfield, Collected Poems*, Gainesville, Facsimiles and Reprints.

Levy, W.T. (1960), *William Barnes, The Man and the Poems*, Dorchester, Longmans.

Massingham, H.J. (1942), 'William Barnes', *Time and Tide*, May 16, 408-410.

Motion, A. (1994a), *William Barnes: Selected Poems*, London, Penguin Books.

Motion, A. (1994b), *Times Literary Supplement*, December 16, 17.

Page, N. (1980), *Thomas Hardy*, London, Bell and Hyman.

Patmore, C. (1862), 'William Barnes, The Dorsetshire Poet', MacMillan's Magazine, 6, 154-163.

Ruskin, W. (1862), *Unto this Last*, London, Smith, Elder and Co.

Scott, L. (pseudonym for Lucy Baxter, Barnes's daughter) (1887), *The Life of William Barnes, Poet and Philologist*, London, Macmillan.

Shepherd, V. (1990), *Language Variety and the Art of the Everyday*, London, Pinter.

Sisson,C.H. (1965), *Art and Action*, London, Methuen.

Smiles, S. (1859), *Self-Help*, London, John Murray.

Sutton, M.K. (1979), 'Truth and the Pastor's Vision in George Crabbe, William Barnes, and R.S. Thomas', in *Survivals of Pastoral*, edited by Richard F. Hardin, Lawrence, University of Kansas Publications, 35-59.

Unwin, R. (1954), *The Rural Muse*, London, Allen and Unwin.

Wright,W. A. (1870), 'Provincial Glossary', *Notes and Queries*, March 12, 271.

Wrigley, C. (1984), *William Barnes: The Dorset Poet*, Wimborne, Dovecote Press.

Young, R. (1868), *New Recitations for Bands of Hope*, Camberwell.

Zietlow, P. (1969), 'Thomas Hardy and William Barnes: Two Dorset Poets', *Proceedings of the Modern Language Association*, 84, 291-303.

Glossary

(Adapted from 'A list of some Dorset words, with a few hints on Dorset word-shapes ' [Barnes, 1879, pp. 459-67]).

The main sounds
1. *ee* in beet.
2. *e* in Dorset (a sound between 1 and 3.)
3. *a* in mate.
4. *i* in birth.
5. *a* in father.
6. *aw* in awe.
7. *o* in dote.
8. *oo* in rood.

In Dorset words which are forms of book-English ones, the Dorset words differ from the others mainly by Grimm's law, that 'likes shift into likes,' and I have given a few hints by which the putting of an English heading for the Dorset one will give the English word. If the reader is posed by *dreaten*, he may try for *dr*, *thr*, which will bring out *threaten*. See *Dr* under *D*. Note: the numbers (as 5, 1) refer to the foregiven table.

a in father, and *au* in daughter are, in "Blackmore," often *a* = 3. So king Alfred gives a legacy to his *yldsta dehter* — oldest daehter. *a* is a fore-eking to participles of a fore time, as *a-vound*; also for the Anglo-Saxon *an*, *in* or *on*, as *a-huntèn* for *an huntunge*.

ag, often for *eg*, as bag, agg, beg, egg.

aï, aÿ (5, 1), Maïd, Maÿ.

Amper, pus.

Anewst, Anighst, very near, or nearly.

A'ra, ever a, as.

Ar a dog, ever a dog.

A'r'n, e'er a one.

A-stooded, A-stogged (as a waggon), with wheels sunk fast into rotten ground.

A-stocked, with feet stuck fast in clay.

A-strout, stiff stretched.

A-thirt (*th* soft), athwart.

A-vore, afore, before.

Ax, ask.

Axan, ashes (of fire).

A-ʒew, dry, milkless.

Backbran' (brand), *Backbron'* (brond), A big brand or block of wood put on the back of the fire.

Ballywrag, scold.

Bandy, a long stick with a bent end to beat abroad cow-dung.

Barken, Barton, a stack-yard or cowyard.

Bavèn, a faggot of long brushwood.

Beä'nhan' (1, 3, 5), bear in hand, uphold or maintain, as an opinion or otherwise.

Beät (I, 4), up, to beat one's way up.

Bennets, flower-stalks of grass.

Be'th, birth.

Bibber, to shake with cold. (This is a Friesic and not an Anglo- Saxon form of the word, and Halbertsma, in his "Lexicon Frisicum," gives it, among others, as a token that Frisians came into Wessex with the Saxons. *See* Eltrot.)

Bissen, thou bist not.

Bittle, a beetle.

Blatch, black stuff; smut.

Blather, a bladder.

Bleäre (I, 3), to low as a cow.

Blind-buck o' Davy, blindman's buff.

Bloodywarrior, the ruddy Stock gilliflower.

Blooèns, blossoms.

Blooth, blossom in the main.

Bluevinny, blue mouldy.

Brack, a breach. ("Neither brack nor crack in it.")

Bran', a brand.

Brantèn, brazen-faced.

Bring-gwaïn (Bring-going), to bring one on his way.

Brocks, broken pieces (as of food).

Bron', a brand.

Bruckly, Bruckle, brittle.

Bundle, to bound off; go away quickly.

Bu'st, burst.

Caddle, a muddle; a puzzling plight amid untoward things, such that a man knows not what to do first.

Car, to carry.

Cassen, casn, canst not.

Chanker, a wide chink.

Charlick, charlock, field-mustard; *Sinapis arvensis.*

Charm, a noise as of many voices.

Choor, a chare, a (weekly) job as of house work.

Chuck, to throw underhanded to a point, or for a catch.

Clack, Clacker, a bird-clacker; a bird-boy's clacking tool, to fray away birds; also the tongue.

Clavy, clavy bwoard, the mantel-shelf.

Clèden, cleavers, goosegrass; *Galium aparine.*

Clips, to clasp.

Clitty, clingy.

Clocks, ornaments on the ankles of stockings.

Clom', clomb, climbed.

Clote, the yellow water-lily; *Nuphar lutea.*

Clout, a blow with the flat hand.

Clum, to handle clumsily.

Cluster o' vive (cluster of five), the fist or hand with its five fingers; wording taken from a cluster of nuts.

Cockle, Cuckle, the bur of the burdock.

Cockleshell, snail shell.

Colepexy, to glean the few apples left on the tree after intaking.

Coll (7), to embrace the neck.

Conker, the hip, or hep; the fruit of the briar.

Cothe, coath (*th* soft), a disease of sheep, the plaice or flook, a flat worm *Distoma nepaticum* in the stomach.

Cou'den, could not.

Coussen, coossen, coosn, couldest not

Craze, to crack a little.

Critch, a big pitcher.

Crock, an iron cooling-pot.

Croodle, to crow softly.

Croop, Croopy-down, to bend down the body; to stoop very low.

Crope, crept.

Crowshell, shell of the fresh-water mussel, as taken out of the river for food by crows.

Cubby-hole, Cubby-house, between the father's knees.

Culvey, the wood pigeon.

Cutty, Cut, the kittywren.

Cwein, cwoin (4, 1), coin.

Cwoffer (8, 4, 4), a coffer.

Dadder, dather, dudder, to maze or bewilder.

Dag, childag, a chilblain.

Dake, to ding or push forth.

Daps, the very likeness, as that of a cast from the same mould.

Dather, see Dadder.

Dent, a dint.

Dewberry, a big kind of blackberry.

Dibs, coins; but truly, the small knee bones of a sheep used in the game of Dibs.

Didden (didn), did not.

Do, the *o,* when not under a strain of voice, is (4) as *e* in 'the man' or as *e* in the French *le.*

Dod, a dump.

Dogs, andirons.

Don, to put on.

Doust, dust.

dr for *thr* in some words, as Drash, thresh.

Drashel, threshold.

Drean, Drène (2), to drawl.

Dreaten, threaten.

Dree, three.

Dringe, Drunge, to throng; push as in a throng.

Droat, throat.

Drong, throng; also a narrow way.

Drough, through.

Drow, throw.

Drub, throb.

Drush, thrush.

Drust, thrust.

Drève (2), drive.

Duck, a darkening, dusk.

Dumbledore, the humble bee.

Dummet, dusk.

Dunch, dull of hearing, or mind

Dunch-nettle, the dead nettle, *Lamium.*

Dunch-pudden, pudding of bare dough.

Dungpot, a dungcart.

Dunt, to blunten as an edge or pain.

Durns, the side posts of a door.

E long itself alone has mostly the Dorset sound (2).

e is put in before s after st, as nestes, nests, vistes, fists.

eä (1, 4) for ea, with the *a* unsounded as lead, mead, leäd, meäd.

eä (I, 3) for the long *a*, 3, as in lade, made, leäde, meäde.

ea of one sound (2) as meat. The two sundry soundings of *ea* 2 and 3 do not go by our spelling *ea* for both, but have come from earlier forms of the words. After a roof letter it may stay as it is, a roof letter, as madden, madd'n; rotten, rott'n. So with *en* for him, tell en, tell'n.

en—not *èn*—in Dorset, as well as in book English, as an ending of some kinds of words often, in running talk, loses the *e*, and in some cases shifts into a sound of the kind of the one close before it. After a lip-letter it becomes a lip-letter *m*, as Rub en, Rub him; rub'n, rub'm; oven, ov'm; open, op'n op'm, in Dorset mostly oben, ob'n, ob'm. So after *f*, deafen, deaf'n, deaf'm, heaven, heav'n, heav'm, in Dorset sometimes heab'm; zeven, zeb'n, zeb'm. After a throat-letter it becomes a throat one, *ng*, as token, tok'n, tok'ng. The *en* sometimes at the end of words means not, as bisse'n, bist not; coust'en, cous'n, could'st not; I didd'n, I did not; diss'n, didst not; hadd'n, had not; muss'n, must not; midd'n, mid not; should'n, should not; 'tis'n, 'tis not; would'n, would not.

Eagrass, aftermath.

Eltrot, Eltroot, cowparsley (*Myrrhis*). (Elt is Freisic, robustus, vegetus, as cowparsley is among other kinds. *See* Bibber.)

Emmet, an ant.

Emmetbut, an anthill.

En, him; A.-Saxon, *hine*.

Èn, for ing, zingèn, singing.

Eve, to become wet as a cold stone floor from thickened steam in some weather.

Evet, eft, newt.

Exe, an axle.

Fakket, a faggot.

Fall, autumn; to fall down is *vall*.

Faÿ (5, I) to speed, succeed.

Feäst (I, 4), a village wake or festival; *festa*.

Flag, a water plant.

Flinders, flying pieces of a body smashed; "Hit it all to flinders."

Flounce, a flying fall as into water.

Flout, a flinging, or blow of one.

Flush, fledged.
Footy, unhandily little.

Gally, to frighten, fray.
Gee, jee, to go, fit, speed.
Giddygander, the meadow orchis.
Gil'cup, gilt cup, the buttercup.
Girt, great.
Glene (2), to smile sneeringly.
Glutch, to swallow.
Gnang, to mock one with jaw waggings, and noisy sounds.
Gnot, a gnat.
Goo, go.
Goocoo flower, Cardamine pratensis.
Goodnow, goodn'er, good neighbour; my good friend; "No, no; not I,
    goodnow;" "No, no; not I, my good friend."
Goolden chaïn, the laburnum.
Gout, an underground gutter.
Graegle, greygle, the wild hyacinth, *Hyacinthus nonscriptus.*
Gramfer, grandfather.
Ground-ash, an ash stick that springs from the ground, and so is tough;
    "Ground the pick," to put the stem of it on the ground, to raise a
    pitch of hay.
Gwoad (8, 4), a goad.

Hacker, a hoe.
Hagrod, hagridden in sleep, if not under the nightmare.
Haïn (5, I), to fence in ground or shut up a field for mowing.
Ha'me, see Hau'm.
Hangèn, sloping ground.
Hansel, Handsel, a hand gift.
Hansel, Handsel, to use a new thing for the first time.
Happer, to hop up as hailstones or rain-drops from ground or pavement
    in a hard storm, or as down-shaken apples; to fall so hard as to hop
    up at falling.
Haps, a hasp.
Ha'skim, halfskim cheese of milk skimmed only once.
Hassen, hast not.
Haum, Haulm, Hulm, the hollow stalks of plants. *Teätie haum,* potato stalks.
Hatch, a low wicket or half door.

Haÿmeäkèn, haymaking. The steps of haymaking by hand, in the rich meadow lands of Blackmore, ere machines were brought into the field, were these: The grass being mown, and lying in *swath*, it was (1) *tedded*, spread evenly over the ground; (2) it was *turned* to dry the under side; (3) it was in the evening raked up into *rollers*, each roller of the grass of the stretch of one rake, and the rollers were sometimes put up into hay cocks; (4) in the morning the rollers were cast abroad into *pa'sels* (parcels) or broad lists, with clear ground between each two: (5) the parcels were turned, and when dry they were pushed up into weäles (weales) or long ridges, and, with a fear of rain, the weäles were put up into *pooks*, or big peaked heaps, the waggon (often called the *plow*) came along between two weäles or rows of pooks, with two loaders, and a pitcher on each side pitched up to them the hay of his side, while two women raked after plow, or raked up the leavings of the pitchers, who stepped back from time to time to take it from them.

Hazen, to forebode.

Hazzle, hazel.

Heal (2), hide, to cover.

Heal (pease), to hoe up the earth on them.

Heän (1, 4), a haft, handle.

Heft, weight.

Herence, hence.

Here right, here on the spot, etc.

Het, heat, also a heat in running.

Het, to hit.

Heth, a hearth, a heath.

Hick, to hop on one leg.

Hidelock, Hidlock, a hiding place. "He is in hidelock." He is absconded.

Hidybuck, hide-and-seek, the game.

Hile of Sheaves, ten, 4 against 4 in a ridge, and 1 at each end.

Ho, to feel misgiving care.

Hodmadod, a little dod or dump; in some parts of England a snail.

Holm, ho'me, holly.

Hook, to gore as a cow.

Honeyzuck, honeysuckle.

Ho'se, hoss, a board on which a ditcher may stand in a wet ditch.

Ho'se-tinger, the dragon-fly, *Libellula*. *Horse* does not mean a horse, but is an adjective meaning coarse or big of its kind, as in horse-radish, or horse-chesnut; most likely the old form of the word gave name to the horse as the big beast where there was not an elephant or other greater one. The dragon-fly is, in some parts, called the "tanging ether" or tanging adder, from *tang*, a long thin body, and a sting. Very few Dorset folk believe that the dragon-fly stings horses any more than that the horse eats horse brambles or horse-mushrooms.

Hud, a pod, a hood-like thing.

Huddick (hoodock), a fingerstall.

Hull, a pod, a hollow thing.

Humbuz, a notched strip of lath, swung round on a string, and humming or buzzing.

Humstrum, a rude, home made musical instrument, now given up.

Jack-o'-lent, a man-like scarecrow. The true Jack-o'-lent was, as we learn from Taylor, the water poet, a ragged, lean-like figure which went as a token of Lent, in olden times, in Lent processions.

Jist, just.

Jut, to nudge or jog quickly.

Kag, a keg.

Kapple cow, a cow with a white muzzle.

Kern, to grow into fruit.

Ketch, katch, to thicken or harden from thinness, as melted fat.

Kecks, kex, a stem of the hemlock or cowparsley.

Keys, (2), the seed vessels of the sycamore.

Kid, a pod, as of the pea.

Kittyboots, low uplaced boots, a little more than ankle high.

Knap, a hillock, a head, or knob (2), a knob-like bud, as of the potato. "The teaties be out in knap."

Laïter (5, I), one run of laying of a hen.

Leän (I, 4), to lean.

Leäne (I, 3), a lane.

Leäse (1, 4), to glean.

Leäse (I, 4), *leaze,* an unmown field, stocked through the Spring and Summer.

Leer, leery, empty.

Lence, a loan, a lending.

Levers, livers, the corn flag.

Lew, sheltered from cold wind.

Lewth, lewness.

Libbets, loose-hanging rags.

Limber, limp.

Linch, linchet, a ledge on a hill-side.

Litsome, lightsome, gay.

Litty, light and brisk of body.

Lo't (7), loft, an upper floor.

Lowl, to loll loosely.

Lumper, a loose step.

Maesh (2), *mesh*, (Blackmore) moss, also a hole or run of a hare, fox, or other wild animal.

Mammet, an image, scarecrow.

Marrels, merrels, the game of nine men's morris.

Mawn, man, (5) a kind of basket.

Meäden (I, 4), stinking chamomile.

Ment (2), to imitate, be like.

Mesh (2), moss.

Mid, might.

Miff, a slight feud, a tiff.

Min (2), observe. You must know.

Mither ho, come hither. A call to a horse on the road.

Moot, the bottom and roots of a felled tree.

More, a root, taproot.

Muggy, misty, damp (weather).

Na'r a, never a (man).

Nar'n, never a one.

N'eet, not yet.

Nesh (2), soft.

Nesthooden, a hooding over a bird's nest, as a wren's.

Netlèns, a food of a pig's inwards tied in knots.

Never'stide, never at all.

Nicky, a very small fagot of sticks.

Nippy, hungry, catchy.

Nitch, a big fagot of wood; a load; a fagot of wood which custom allows a hedger to carry home at night.

Not (hnot or knot), hornless.

Nother, neither (adverb).

Nunch, a nog or knob of food.

Nut (of a wheel), the stock or nave.

O', of.

O'm (2), of em, them.

O'n (2), of him.

or. See *R.*

O's (2), of us.

Orts, leavings of hay put out in little heaps in the fields for the cows.

Over-right, opposite.

Oves, eaves.

Paladore, a traditional name of Shaftesbury, the British *Caer Paladr*, said by British history to have been founded by *Rhun Paladr-bras*, 'Rhun of the stout spear.'

Pank, pant.

Par, to shut up close; confine.

Parrick, a small enclosed field; a paddock—but paddock was an old word for a toad or frog.

Pa'sels, parcels. See Haÿmeäkèn.

Peärt (1, 4), pert; lively.

Pease, Peeze (2), to ooze.

Peewit, the lapwing.

Pitch. See Haÿmeäkèn.

Plesh (2), *Plush* (a hedge), to lay it. To cut the stems half off and peg them down on the bank where they sprout upward. To plush, shear, and trim a hedge are sundry handlings of it.

Plim, to swell up.

Plock, a hard block of wood.

Plow, a waggon, often so called. The plough or plow for ploughing is the Zull.

Plounce, a strong plunge.

Pluffy, plump.

Pont, to hit a fish or fruit, so as to bring on a rotting.

Pooks. See Haÿmeäkèn.

Popple, a pebble.

Praïse (5, I), prize, to put forth or tell to others a pain or ailing. "I had a risèn on my eärm, but I didden *praïse* it," say anything about it.

ps for *sp* in clasp, claps; hasp, haps; wasp, waps.

Pummy, pomice.

Quaer, queer.

Quag a quaking bog.

Quar, a quarry.

Quarrel, a square window pane.

Quid, a cud.

Quirk, to grunt with the breath without the voice.

R, at the head of a word, is strongly breathed, as *Hr* in Anglo-Saxon, as *Hhrong*, the rong of a ladder. *R* is given in Dorset by a rolling of the tongue back under the roof. *R* before *s*, *st*, and *th* often goes out, as bu'st, burst; ve'ss, verse; be'th, birth; cu'st, curst; fwo'ce, force; me'th, mirth. For *or*, as an ending sometimes given before a free breathing, or *h*, try *ow*,—hollor, hollow.

Raft, to rouse, excite.

Rake, to reek.

Ram, Rammish, rank of smell.

Rammil, raw milk (cheese), of unskimmed milk.

Ramsclaws, the creeping crowfoot, *Ranunculus repens*.

Randy, a merry uproar or meeting.

Rangle, to range or reach about.

Rathe, early; whence rather.

Ratch, to stretch.

Readship, criterion, counsel.

Reämes (1, 3), skeleton, frame.

Reän (I, 4), to reach in greedily in eating.

Reäves, a frame of little rongs on the side of a waggon.

Reed (2), wheat hulm drawn for thatching.

Reely, to dance a reel.

Reem, to stretch, broaden.

Rick, a stack.

Rig, to climb about.

Rivel, shrivel; to wrinkle up.

Robin Hood, The Red campion.

Roller (6, 4). See Haÿmeäkèn. A Roller was also a little roll of wool from the card of a woolcomber.

Rottlepenny, the yellow rattle. *Rhinanthus Crista-galli*.

Rouet, a rough tuft of grass.

Sammy, soft, a soft head; simpleton.

Sar, to serve or give food to (cattle).

Sarch, to search.

Scrag, a crooked branch of a tree.

Scraggle, to screw scramly about (of a man), to screw the limbs scramly as from rheumatism.

Scram, distorted, awry.

Scroff, bits of small wood or chips, as from windfalls or hedge plushing.

Scroop, to skreak lowly as new shoes or a gate hinge.

Scote, to shoot along fast in running.

Scud, a sudden or short down-shooting of rain, a shower.

Scwo'ce, chop or exchange.

Settle, a long bench with a high planken back.

Shard, a small gap in a hedge.

Sharps, shafts of a waggon.

Shatten, shalt not.

Shroud (trees), to cut off branches.

Sheeted cow, with a broad white band round her body.

Shoulden (shoodn), should not.

Shrow, Sh'ow, Sh'ow crop, the shrew mouse.

Skim, skimmy, grass; to cut off rank tuffs, or rouets.

Slaït, (5, I), *Slite*, a slade, or sheep run.

Slent, a tear in clothes.

Slidder, to slide about.

Slim, sly.

Sloo, sloe.

Slooworm, the slow-worm.

Smame, to smear.

Smeech, a cloud of dust.

Smert, to smart; pain.

Snabble, to snap up quickly.

Snags, small pea-big sloes, also stumps.

Sneäd (1, 4), a scythe stem.

Snoatch, to breathe loudly through the nose.

Snoff, a snuff of a candle.

Sock, a short loud sigh.

Sowel, zowel, a hurdle stake.

Sparbill, Sparrabill, a kind of shoe nail.

Spars, forked sticks used in thatching.

Speaker (1, 4), a long spike of wood to bear the hedger's nitch on his shoulder.

Spears, speers, the stalks of reed grass.

Spik, spike, lavender.

Sprack, active.

Sprethe (2), to chap as of the skin, from cold.

Spry, springy in leaping, or limb work.

Spur (dung), to cast it abroad.

Squail (5, 1), to fling something at a bird or ought else.

Squot, to flatten by a blow.

Staddle, a bed or frame for ricks.

Staïd (5, 1) steady, oldish.

Stannèns, stalls in a fair or market.

Steän (1, 4) (a road), to lay it in stone.

Steärt (1, 4), a tail or outsticking thing.

Stitch (of corn), a conical pile of sheaves.

Stout, the cowfly, *Tabantus.*

Strawèn, a strewing. All the potatoes of one mother potato.

Strawmote, a straw or stalk.

Streech, an outstretching (as of a rake in raking); a-strout stretched out stiffly
like frozen linen.

Strent, a long slent or tear.

Stubbard, a kind of apple.

Stunpoll (7), stone head, blockhead; also an old tree almost dead.

Tack, a shelf on a wall.

Taffle, to tangle, as grass or corn beaten down by storms. *Taït,* to play at
see-saw.

Tamy (3, I), *tammy* (5, I), tough, that may be drawn out in strings, as rich
toasted cheese.

Teäve, (1, 3), to reach about strongly as in work or a struggle.

Teery, tewly, weak of growth.

Tewly, weakly.

th is soft (as *th* in thee), as a heading of these words:—thatch, thief, thik,
thimble, thin, think, thumb.

Theäse, this or these.

Theasum (1, 4), these.

Tidden (tidn), it is not.

Tilty, touchy, irritable.

Timmersome, restless.

Tine, to kindle, also to fence in ground.

Tistytosty, a toss ball of cowslip blooms.

To-year, this year (as to-day).
Tranter, a common carrier.
Trendel, a shallow tub.
Tump, a little mound.
Tun, the top of the chimney above the roof ridge.
Tut (work), piecework.
Tutty, a nosegay.
Tweil (4, 1), toil.
Twite, to twit reproach.

Unheal, uncover, unroof.

v is taken for *f* as the heading of some purely English words, as vall, fall, vind, find.
Veag, *Veg* (2), a strong fit of anger.
Vern, fern.
Ve'se, vess, a verse.
Vinny cheese, cheese with fen or blue-mould.
Vitty, nice in appearance.
Vlanker, a flake of fire.
Vlee, fly.
Vo'k, folk.
Vooty, unhandily little.
Vuz̧, Vuz̧z̧en, furze, gorse.

Wag, to stir.
Wagwanton, quaking grass.
Weäle (I, 3), a ridge of dried hay; see Haÿmeäkèn.
Weäse (1, 4), a pad or wreath for the head under a milkpail.
Welshnut, a walnut.
Werden, were not or was not.
Wevet, a spider's w-eb.
Whicker, to neigh.
Whindlèn, weakly, small of growth.
Whiver, to hover, quiver.
Whog, go off; to a horse.
Whur, to fling overhanded.
Wi', with.
Widdicks, withes or small brushwood.
Wink, a winch; crank of a well.

Withwind, the bindweed.

wo (8, 4), for the long o, 7, as bwold, bold; cwold, cold.

Wont, a mole.

Wops, wasp. *ps*, not *sp*, in Anglo-Saxon, and now in Holstein.

Wotshed, *Wetshod*, wet-footed.

Wride, to spread out in growth.

Wride, the set of stems or stalks from one root or grain of corn.

Writh, a small wreath of tough wands, to link hurdles to the sowels (stakes).

Wrix, wreathed or wattle work, as a fence.

Yop, yelp.

z for *s* as a heading of some, not all, pure Saxon words, nor for *s* of
   inbrought foreign words.

Zand, sand.

Zennit, *zennight*, seven night; "This day zennit."

Zew, *azew*, milkless.

Zive, a scythe.

Zoo, so.

Zull (a plough), to plough ground.

Zwath, a swath.

148

Index of titles and first lines